It's Number Time!

by
Lynette Pyne

Carson-Dellosa Publishing Company, Inc.
Greensboro, North Carolina

Dedication
to my family, Ed, Megan, and Jake

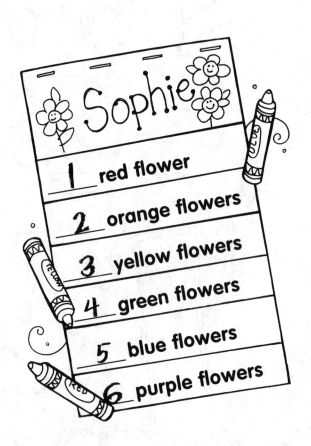

Credits
Editor: Ashley Anderson
Layout Design: Van Harris and Mark Conrad
Inside Illustrations: Janet Armbrust
Cover Design: Peggy Jackson
Cover Illustrations: Dan Sharp

ISBN 1-59441-954-X

Table of Contents

Introduction & Icon Key

It's Number Time! includes over 100 theme-based activities to practice early math skills. Each theme contains several activities that focus on beginning skills, such as counting and number recognition, as well as more advanced skills, such as matching numbers and sets.

Skills and topics of focus include:

* Counting
* Number recognition
* Matching
* Sets

* Patterning and sorting
* Sequencing and number order
* Writing numbers
* Comparing

* Graphing
* Shapes
* Addition and subtraction
* Calendar and time

It's Number Time! is designed for use with any early childhood curriculum. The activities can supplement a themed unit or can be selected by skill. Skills are incorporated into fun activities, like classroom games, songs, and crafts; and many of the activities can be adapted for whole-group, small-group, or individual play. Most activities suggest using numbers from 0 to 10, but they can easily be adapted to use a larger or smaller range of numbers depending on students' needs. Also, convenient icons are provided to designate the skills of focus for each activity. A reference index sorted by skill and a suggested literature list for expanding the classroom library are also included.

So, what are you waiting for? 1 . . . 2 . . . 3 . . . *It's Number Time!*

Caution: Some activities require a variety of small objects and manipulatives. Remember that small pieces may present a choking hazard for young children. Select manipulatives and game pieces according to students' needs. Also, before completing any food activity, ask families' permission and inquire about students' food allergies and religious or other preferences.

Skills for each activity are denoted by the following icons:

Icon	Skill	Icon	Skill	Icon	Skill
1²3	Counting	ABAB	Patterning and Sorting	(graph)	Graphing
(eyes)	Number Recognition	1st	Sequencing and Number Order	(shapes)	Shapes
(dominoes 2)	Matching	(pencil)	Writing Numbers	+/-	Addition and Subtraction
(dots)	Sets	(circles)	Comparing	(clock)	Calendar and Time

100th Day of School

100th Day Pattern ✍ ABAB ....

Use this activity to help students count the first 100 days of school while practicing patterning skills. Create a supply of colorful shapes from construction paper. Laminate the shapes for durability. At the beginning of each day, attach one shape to a sentence strip and number the shape. Each day, add one more shape to create a simple pattern. Ask students which shape to put on the sentence strip to continue the pattern. When a strip has 10 shapes on it, begin a new strip with a new pattern. Continue the process until there are 10 sentence strips with 10 shapes on each one. The last shape will mark the 100th day of school!

100 Collections 1²³ ∴ ....

Give each student a resealable plastic bag to fill with 100 of the same item. Send each student home with a plastic bag and a note explaining the project. Remind students that all 100 items must fit into their bags. Ask families to help the students collect items and count them in groups of 10. Suggest small items, such as paper clips, dried pasta, dried beans, or pennies. On the 100th day of school, have students bring their bags to class and work together in small groups to count their objects. Display the collections on a table to give students an idea of what 100 looks like.

Tasty 100 Necklaces 1²³ ∴ ....

This colorful "jewelry" will make any 100th day celebration extra fun. Give each student a piece of yarn to make a necklace and an empty bowl. Divide the class into small groups and give each group 10 small paper cups and a bowl of colorful ring cereal. Let students take turns counting and placing 10 pieces of ring cereal into each cup. When a student has 10 pieces of cereal in each cup, have her pour the cereal into her bowl and pass the cups to the next member of the group. Then, let her thread her 100 pieces of cereal onto the piece of yarn. Help each student tie the ends of her necklace together. Students can wear the necklaces during the class's 100th day of school celebration.

Special 100th Day Snack 1²³ ∴ ....

Have students work in small groups to make tasty 100th day of school snacks. Give each group a snack food, such as ring cereal, candy-covered chocolates, chocolate chips, raisins, jelly beans, gumdrops, or nuts. Let each group work together to count 10 groups of 10 (a total of 100) of their snack item. When all of the groups have 100 pieces, mix all of the types of snacks together in a large bowl. Scoop the mix into small cups and let students enjoy a special treat.

100th Day Posters 1²3 ∴

As the 100th day of school approaches, start collecting items to make 100th day posters. Examples of items to use include cotton balls, craft pom-poms, craft sticks, buttons, paper clips, stickers, individually wrapped candies, etc. When the 100th day of school arrives, have each student make a poster to represent the number 100. (Or, have students work together in small groups.) Encourage each student (or group) to count 10 groups of 10 (a total of 100) items. Students can glue the items directly onto the posters or place them in small, resealable plastic bags that can be stapled to the posters. Hang the posters around the room for everyone to enjoy on the 100th day of school.

Hurry to 100 Game 1²3

Set up a math center to show students that they can count to 100. Create a grid with 100 squares on it in 10 rows and 10 columns. Make copies of the grid so that each student who visits the center will have a copy. Place the grids and a fair number cube on the table. Students will also need a method of marking their grids, such as stickers to place over the squares or crayons or markers to fill in the squares. To play the game, the first player rolls the cube, counts the number of dots shown, and covers or fills in the matching number of squares on his grid. Then, the second player takes a turn. Play continues until one player fills his entire grid of 100 squares.

How Much Is 100? 1²3 ∴

This class activity will help students see what 100 really looks like. Provide a large container of paper clips. Have each student count 5 paper clips and connect them to create a short chain. (If you have fewer than 20 students, you should create your own chain consisting of the number of paper clips needed to make 100.) Then, have each student connect her chain to a classmate's chain and continue this process until one long class chain is created. Display the paper clip chain on a 100th day of school bulletin board.

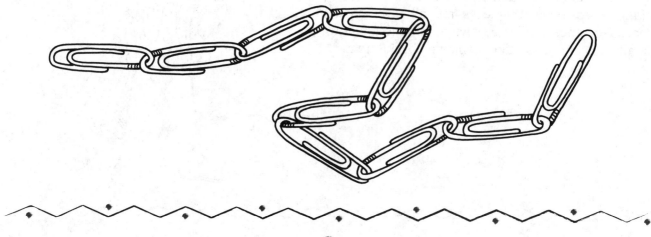

6

Birthdays

Birthday Surprises

Program 11 birthday paper plates with a number from 0 to 10. Provide a supply of birthday-themed stickers and solid-colored paper napkins. Students can play this game independently or with partners. To play, a student reads and identifies the number on a paper plate and then places the matching number of stickers on a paper napkin. Play continues until the student has made a sticker set for each plate.

Birthday Wishes

On a piece of graph paper, use colorful markers to draw a simple birthday cake with candles on top (a large rectangle with lines representing candles). Laminate the graph paper for durability. Place the drawing on a table and provide additional pieces of graph paper and markers or crayons for students. Have each student take a piece of graph paper and copy the original drawing on her paper. Encourage students to count how many squares are colored in each row and column and try to duplicate the drawing exactly.

When Is Your Birthday?

Celebrate classroom birthdays with this graphing activity. Give each student copies of the Birthday Cake and Candle Patterns (page 9) to decorate, cut out, and label with his name. Write each month of the year on a sentence strip. Place the sentence strips in order on the floor to serve as the x-axis of a graph. Or, attach the strips in a row across the bottom of a low bulletin board. Recite the following rhyme in unison with the class:

> *Birthdays, birthdays, all the year through;*
> *Which month has a special day for you?*

Then, name a month. When a student hears his birth month named, have him place his birthday cake in the correct column of the graph. When the graph is complete, help students count aloud how many birthdays are in each month and name which months have the most and fewest birthdays.

Count on Birthday Fun

Make 11 copies of the Birthday Cake Pattern (page 9) on colorful paper. Cut out the patterns and program each cake with a number from 0 to 10. Make 55 copies of the Candle Patterns (page 9) on colorful paper and cut them out. Laminate the cakes and candles for durability. Attach a strip of hook-and-loop tape across the top of each cake. Attach a small piece of hook-and-loop tape to the bottom of the back of each candle. Place all of the pieces at a learning center. Instruct students to choose a birthday cake, read the number, and then place the matching number of candles on the cake. Play continues until each cake is matched with the correct number of candles.

Sequencing, Sorting, and More 1st ABAB

Design a center in which students can practice sequencing, sorting, and creating patterns with a birthday theme. Make copies of the Birthday Cake and Candle Patterns (page 9) on colorful paper. Make sure you have at least two of each pattern in each color. Label the patterns with numbers from 0 to 10. Make at least two copies of each number. Cut out the pieces and laminate them for durability. Encourage students to sort the pieces by color and number, make patterns with the pieces, or sequence the pieces in numerical order. If you wish, have students work with partners. One partner can start a pattern, sort, or numerical sequence, and the other can complete it.

Birthday Concentration

Make one copy of the Birthday Cake and Candle Patterns (page 9) for each student. Write each student's name and birthday on a cake. Write only the matching birthday on a candle. Laminate the pieces for durability. Have players randomly select five students' cakes and candles, shuffle them, and lay them facedown in equal rows. Each player takes a turn flipping over one cake and one candle. He should read the birthdays on the two pieces. If the pieces match, the student gets to keep that pair. If they do not match, they are placed facedown in the same spots, and another player takes her turn. The game ends when all of the pieces have been matched. If desired, have students read the names on the cakes and give the cakes and matching candles to the correct students. Have students repeat the game after reshuffling the pieces or after selecting new cakes and candles.

Birthday Roundup 1st

Make one copy of the Birthday Cake Pattern (page 9) for each student. Then, enlarge the cake pattern and make another copy for each student. Number both sets of cakes and laminate for durability. Tape the large cakes, in numerical order, in a long row along a wall. Place a self-stick note over the number on each cake. Punch holes in the small cakes and tie yarn through the holes to create necklaces. Randomly give each student a necklace. Using only nonverbal communication, have students line themselves up in front of the row of cakes on the wall in numerical order. After they assemble themselves, remove the self-stick notes one at a time to allow students to see if they lined up correctly.

Birthday Cake & Candle Patterns

Activities found on pages 7–8.

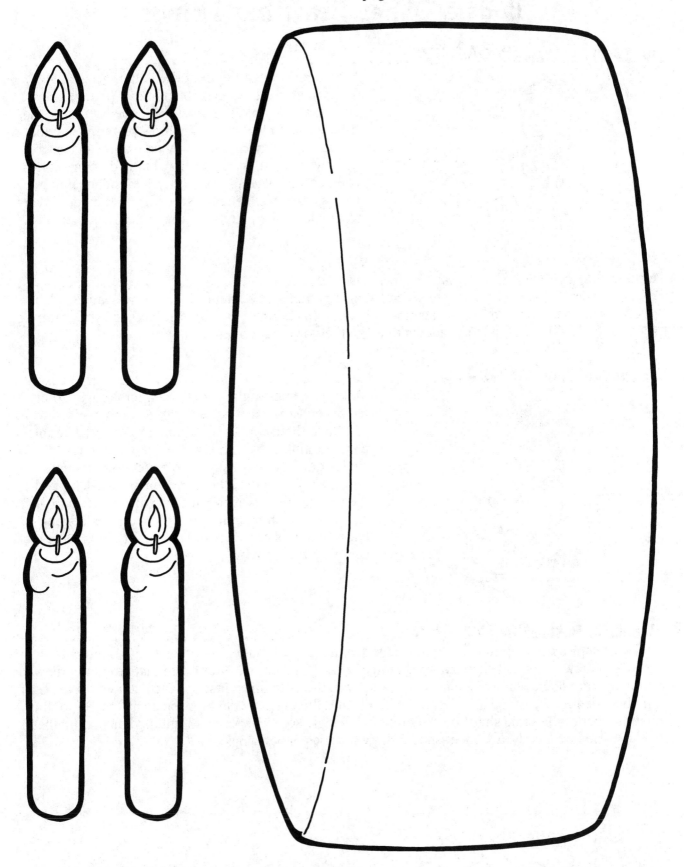

Bugs & Other Crawling Things

Butterfly Patterns ABAB

Make one copy of the Butterfly Pattern (page 13) for each student. Give each student a pattern and a supply of colorful dot stickers. On one butterfly wing, have each student create a simple pattern using the dot stickers. If necessary, provide parameters, such as how many stickers and how many different colors can be used. Then, have students exchange butterflies with classmates. Let each student use the dot stickers to duplicate the pattern on the butterfly's other wing.

Going Buggy! ABAB

Using bug stamps or stickers, create several simple patterns on sentence strips. Have each student select a sentence strip and use the stamps or stickers to continue the pattern. Provide extra stamps or stickers and sentence strips for students to make their own patterns.

Count the Spots 1²3

Make 11 copies of the Ladybug Pattern (page 14) on red paper. Label each pattern with a number from 0 to 10. Laminate the ladybugs for durability. To make counters, paint 55 milk caps with black paint. Or, cut out 55 circles from black construction paper and laminate for durability. To play the game, have a student read the number on a ladybug and use the counters to place the matching number of spots on the ladybug's back. Students can work independently or in pairs to complete this activity.

Beautiful Butterflies

Make 10 copies of the Butterfly Pattern (page 13). Label each butterfly's body with a number from 1 to 10 and draw one small shape, approximately 1" x 1" (2.5 cm x 2.5 cm). Laminate the butterflies for durability. Provide write-on/wipe-away markers with the butterflies. Instruct each student to read the number, identify the shape on a butterfly's body, and then use a write-on/wipe-away marker to draw that number of the same shape on the butterfly's wings. For example, if a butterfly has the number 4 and a circle on its body, a student should draw 4 circles on its wings.

Creeping Along **1**st ....

Use a cute caterpillar to teach number order. Cut out 12 circles from colorful construction paper. Glue one circle on the left side of a piece of poster board and decorate it to resemble a caterpillar's face. Trace 11 circle outlines in a wavy path behind the face to make a caterpillar's body. Label the 11 remaining circle cutouts with numbers from 0 to 10. To play the game, have a student place the circle cutouts in order from 0 to 10 on the poster board to make the caterpillar's body. For an extra challenge, have him put the numbers in reverse order.

Caterpillar Snacks ▮▮▮ 1²3 ◯◯ ....

Read *The Very Hungry Caterpillar* by Eric Carle (Scholastic, 1994) aloud to students and then use the story to create a pictograph. Draw a grid with five columns on a large piece of bulletin board paper. Label each column with the name and a picture of a type of fruit the caterpillar eats in the story (apple, pear, plum, strawberry, and orange). Read the story aloud a second time and have students take turns coloring a square on the graph for each piece of fruit the caterpillar eats. When the graph is finished, have students count aloud how many pieces of fruit the caterpillar ate. Ask questions about the graph that challenge students to judge more, less, most, least, etc. Extend the activity by creating a second graph labeled with the same fruits. Give each student a square of paper and tell her to write her name on it. When called upon, have each student place her square on the graph to indicate which fruit is her favorite.

Spider Shapes ✧ ⊡² ....

On a large piece of poster board, draw a square, a rectangle, a circle, a rhombus, a triangle, and an oval. Be sure to leave plenty of space between the shapes. Make each shape on the poster board into a "spider" by drawing eight legs and a face. For each shape drawn, cut an identical shape from colorful paper. Laminate the poster board and cutouts for durability. Attach hook-and-loop tape to each poster board spider and each shape cutout. To play the game, a student should match each shape cutout to the spider with the same shape and identify the name of the shape.

Just Hanging Around ◡◡ ....

Enlarge and make 11 copies of the Spider Pattern (page 15) on gray construction paper and then cut out the patterns. Program each spider with a number from 0 to 10. Using fishing line, suspend the spiders from the ceiling or tape them high on a wall in random order. Call out a student's name and a number. That student should quickly find the corresponding spider and stand below it.

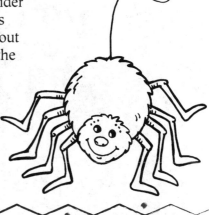

11

Where's My Web?

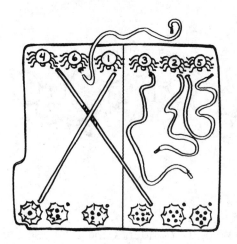

Have students help these spiders find their homes while sharpening their math skills. Make six reduced copies of the Spider Pattern (page 15) and six reduced copies of the Spiderweb Pattern (page 15). Program each spider with a number from 1 to 6. Program each web with a number set from 1 to 6. Attach the spiders in random order along the top of an open file folder and attach the spiderwebs along the bottom. Punch a hole directly to the right of each spider and each web. Cut six pieces of different colors of yarn and thread each one through the hole beside a spider pattern. Tape the yarn to the back of the folder to secure it in place. To play the game, a student should find each spider's matching web and thread its piece of yarn through the hole beside the web, continuing until all pieces have been matched. Make the game self-checking by color coding the back of the folder according to the colors of the yarn.

Spin a Web of Spiders

Enlarge and make two copies of the Spiderweb Pattern (page 15). Reduce and make 20 copies of the Spider Pattern (page 15). Laminate and cut out all of the patterns. Put the spiderwebs on a table and place a few spiders on one of the webs. Place the remaining spider patterns nearby. According to your directions, a student should place a set of spiders on the empty web that is greater than, less than, or equal to the other set. Continue playing by clearing the spider patterns from one of the webs and giving students instructions about creating new sets. You can also let students play this game in pairs. Have one partner create the first set and give the instructions. Then, students may switch roles after the second partner has followed the directions.

Silly Spiders ABAB

Reduce and make several copies of the Spider Pattern (page 15) each on four different colors of paper. Then, enlarge the pattern and make several copies each on the same colors of paper. Cut out all of the patterns, laminate for durability, and place them in a resealable plastic bag. Attach four copies of the Spiderweb Pattern (page 15) to a piece of poster board to make a game board. To play the game, a student should sort the spiders by color onto the spiderwebs or sort them by size onto two of the spiderwebs.

Butterfly Pattern

Activities found on page 10.

Ladybug Pattern

Activity found on page 10.

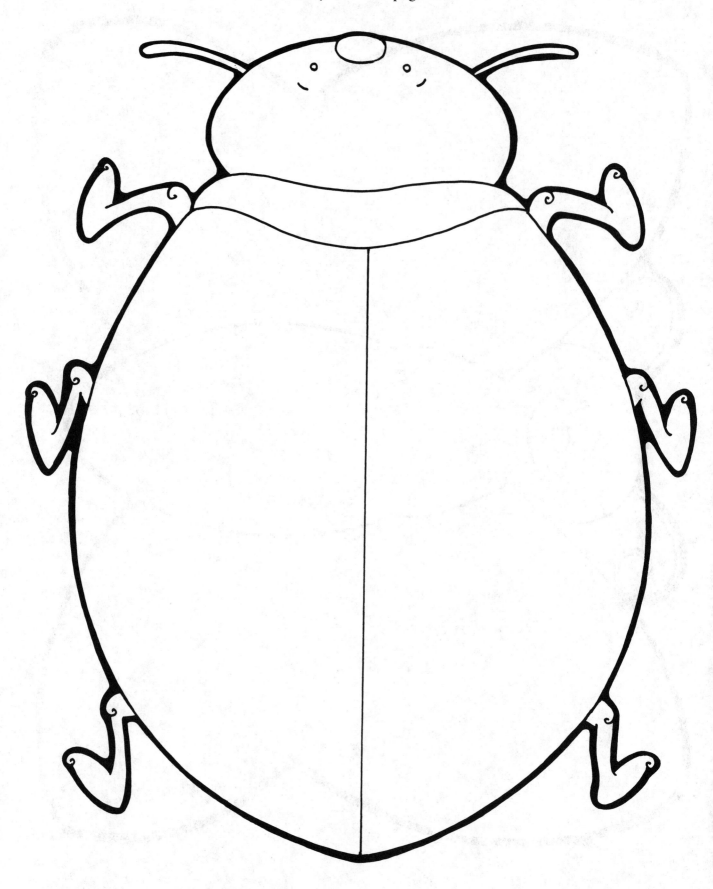

Spider & Spiderweb Patterns

Activities found on pages 11–12.

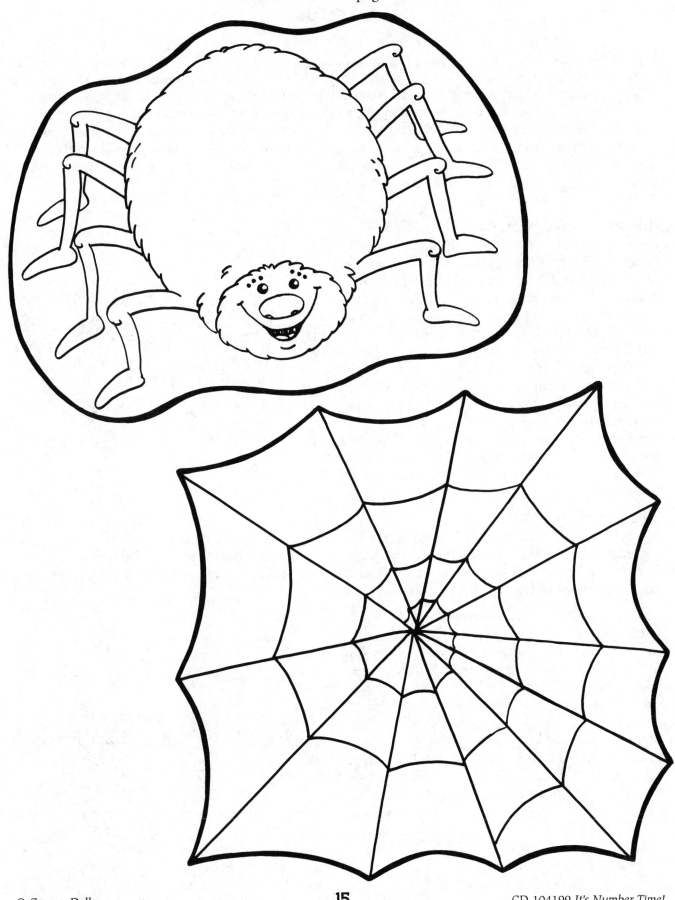

Circus

Sky-High Fun

Make 11 reduced copies of the Balloon Pattern (page 18) and 11 reduced copies of the Clown Pattern (page 18) on colorful paper. Program each balloon with a number set from 0 to 10. Tape or staple a piece of yarn to the bottom of each balloon. Attach the balloons across the top of a piece of poster board in random order. Program each clown with a number from 0 to 10. Attach the clowns across the bottom of the poster board and punch a hole through each clown's left hand. To play, a student reads the number on a clown, finds the matching balloon, and slips the yarn into the clown's hand. Draw lines on the back of the game board for self-checking.

"Elephant-astic" Counting

Copy and cut out 11 reduced copies of the Elephant Patterns (page 19). Program each elephant with a number from 0 to 10. Laminate the elephants for durability. Attach each elephant to a cup or small container. Have a small group of students sit in a row on the floor with the elephant cups lined up in front of them. Provide a bag of packing peanuts for students to use as counters. (If packing peanuts are not available, use dried lima beans or other items that are large enough for young students to handle easily.) Allow students to take turns counting and "feeding" each elephant the correct number of "peanuts." When all of the cups are filled, have students pour the peanuts back into the bag, stand up, switch places, and start again.

Two-Ring Circus

Place two large plastic hoops on the floor. Ask two students to hop inside one hoop and three students to hop inside the other hoop. Ask the rest of the class to decide which hoop has more students and which has fewer. Continue playing by having different numbers of students hop in and out of the hoops to create different groups for comparison.

Clowning Around

Allow students to use their creativity to make shape clown faces. Cut out a class supply of circles, rectangles, squares, and triangles in various sizes and colors. Cut out large white circles for students to use for their clowns' faces. Place the shapes and several glue sticks on a table. Have students make their own unique clown faces by gluing the shapes in different combinations to create facial features, hair, hats, bow ties, and other decorations. Provide craft sticks for students to glue to the backs of their clowns to make puppets or masks.

Who Spilled the Popcorn? 1²3 👀
Provide a bowl of packing peanuts or dried lima beans (to represent popcorn), two small popcorn containers (often available at party supply stores or if you ask at the refreshments counter at a movie theater), a timer, and a spinner. Label the sections of the spinner *0, 1, 2, 3, 4, 5,* and *Spill the popcorn!* Have students play this game in pairs. Give each student a popcorn container and set the timer for five minutes. Players will take turns spinning the spinner. If it lands on a number greater than zero, the player takes that many pieces of "popcorn" from the bowl and puts them in his container. If the spinner lands on *Spill the popcorn!*, he must put all of his popcorn back into the bowl. Let students continue playing until the timer sounds. The student with the most popcorn in his container when time expires is the winner.

Color-By-Number Clown 👀
Create a color-by-number worksheet using the Clown Pattern (page 18). Make an enlarged copy of the pattern and program the sections of the drawing with numbers from 1 to 5. Then, make one copy of the numbered worksheet for each student. To make a color key, write the numbers from 1 to 5 on the board and allow students to decide which color to use for each number. Give each student a worksheet and provide markers or crayons. Let students use the color key to color their clown pictures. Display the colorful clowns around the classroom.

The Right Number of Peanuts 🎲 1²3 ⁙
Reduce and copy 55 Elephant Patterns (page 19). Make sentence strip sets by gluing sets of elephants (from 1 to 10) to 10 sentence strips. If desired, number the elephants on each sentence strip. Provide a container of packing peanuts or dried lima beans. Have a student choose a sentence strip set and "feed" each elephant one "peanut." Have the student count aloud the number of elephants and the number of peanuts in the set before moving on to the next set.

Clown & Balloon Patterns

Activities found on pages 16–17.

CD-104199 *It's Number Time!*

Elephant Patterns

Activities found on pages 16–17.

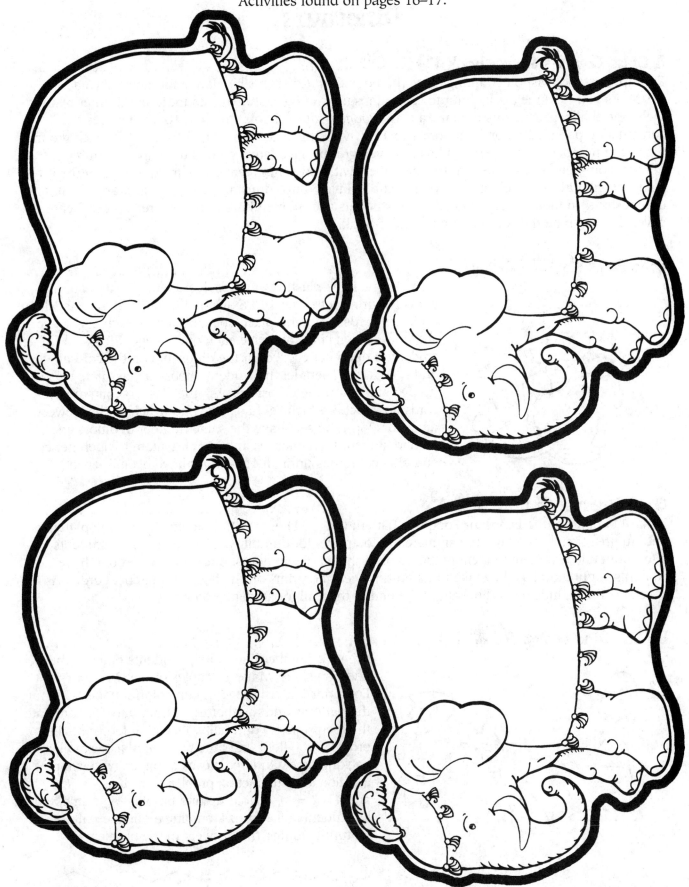

 CD-104199 *It's Number Time!*

Dinosaurs

A Class *Count-A-Saurus* Book 1²3 ∴ 👀

Put a prehistoric twist on counting using the book *Count-a-saurus* by Nancy Blumenthal (Aladdin, 1992). As you read the book, point to each dinosaur and have students count it aloud. After hearing the story, challenge students to make a class *Count-a-saurus* book. Program 10 large pieces of construction paper with numbers from 1 to 10. Divide the class into 10 groups and give each group a piece of numbered paper. (If you have uneven groups, give larger groups the papers with higher numbers on them and smaller groups the papers with lower numbers on them so that all of the students will have more chances to participate.) Have groups draw and color the appropriate number of dinosaurs on their papers. If needed, let students use Blumenthal's book as a reference. Create a cover and combine the pages to make a class book.

Dino Eggs 1²3 ⊙⊙ ∴

Provide one large plastic egg for each student. Create counting cards featuring sets from 1 to 6 using dinosaur stamps or stickers on index cards. Fold and place one card inside each egg. Have students sit in a circle and give each one an egg. Choose a student to open her egg, count the dinosaurs on the card aloud, and hold it up. Then, let the student choose a classmate to open his egg and count the dinosaurs. Ask the class to compare the cards and decide which set has more and which set has fewer dinosaurs, or if the sets have the same number of dinosaurs. The second student then chooses another classmate to open her egg, and play continues until all of the eggs have been opened.

On a Dinosaur Trail 1st 👀 1²3

Make 11 copies of the Dinosaur Footprint Pattern (page 21) on colorful paper. Cut out the patterns and number them from 0 to 10. Laminate the footprints for durability. Give each pair of students a footprint and ask them to identify the number shown. Beginning at one end of the room, have students count aloud as they take turns putting their footprints on the floor in numerical order. As a special surprise, hide a toy dinosaur at the end of the trail for students to find.

Do the Dino Stomp +/- 1st 1²3

Create a number line to help students practice their addition skills. Make 11 copies of the Dinosaur Footprint Pattern (page 21) on colorful paper. Cut out the patterns and number them from 0 to 10. Laminate the footprints for durability. Place the footprints in order on the floor and tape them in place with clear packing tape. On large pieces of paper, write simple addition and subtraction problems, such as *1 + 1 = ___* and *4 − 2 = ___* . Hold up one problem at a time and let students take turns stomping along the path of footprints to find the answers to the problems.

Dinosaur Footprint Pattern

Activities found on page 20.

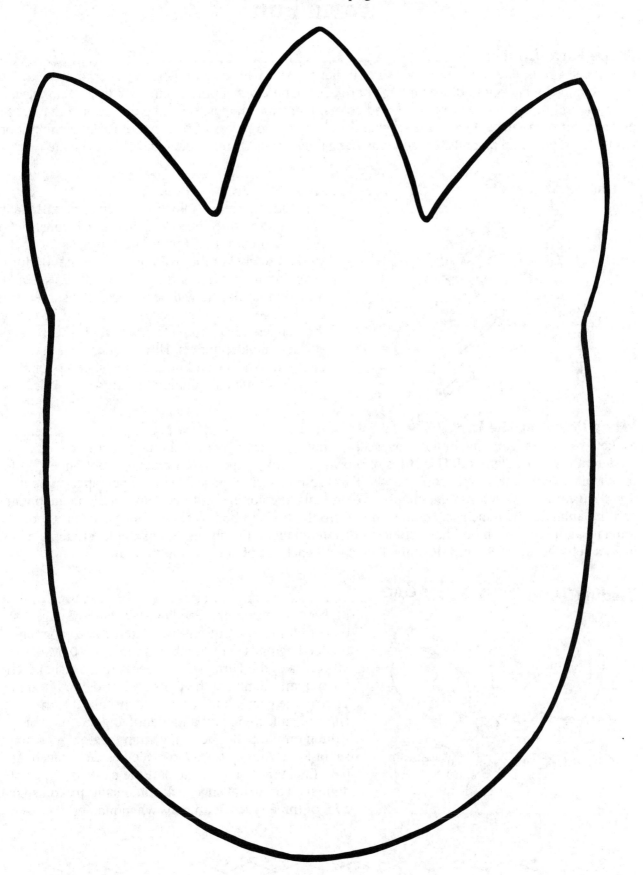

CD-104199 *It's Number Time!*

Farm Fun

Shape Farm Animals

Create a shape farm animal mural. Cover a bulletin board with blue and green paper to make a pasture and sky background. Add a large barn. Cut out a class supply of circles, ovals, rectangles, squares, and triangles in various sizes and colors. Place the shapes, several glue sticks, and pieces of green paper on a table. Have students glue the shapes onto pieces of paper in different combinations to create unique farm animals. Let students hang their animals on the bulletin board to create a mural.

Counting Sheep 1 2 3

Let students create a flock of sheep to count! Have each student trace her hand onto black construction paper and cut it out. Provide cotton balls for each student to glue to the palm area of her handprint. (The thumb of a handprint will be a sheep's head, and the four fingers will be its legs.) Let students use chalk or gel pens to add eyes, noses, and hooves to their sheep. Help students attach their sheep to craft sticks to make puppets. Have students sit in a circle or stand in a row and hold up the sheep puppets as the class counts them aloud in unison.

Who's Down on the Farm? 1 2 3 ABAB

Make a classroom counting mural. Cover a bulletin board with green and blue paper to create a pasture and sky background. Use strips of brown paper to create a fence along the bottom edge of the display. Duplicate several copies of the Farm Animal Cards (page 23) on white paper and cut apart the cards. Let each student choose two animals to color and cut out. Have students help you sort the animals and attach sets of like animals to the bulletin board. Then, count each group of animals aloud in unison and have students dictate a label for each set. For example, students might label a set *9 horses* or *5 sheep*. Post the labels with each set of animals on the mural.

Feeding Time! 1 2 3 ABAB

Make 10 copies of the Feeding Pail Pattern (page 24) on colorful paper. Cut out the patterns and program the feeding pails with numbers from 1 to 10. Make 10 copies of the Farm Animal Cards (page 23) and cut them apart. Laminate the pails and cards for durability. To play the game, have each student take a turn choosing a feeding pail and identifying the number written on the pail. Then, have him create a matching set of Farm Animal Cards to place beside the feeding pail. Encourage students to sort the cards by types of animals. For a challenge, ask students to try to use one, two, or three types of animals when making each set.

Farm Animal Cards

Activities found on page 22.

cow

horse

goose

chicken

sheep

goat

dog

cat

pig

Feeding Pail Pattern

Activity found on page 22.

Nursery Rhymes & Stories

"One, Two, Buckle My Shoe" 1²3  ....

On a piece of chart paper, write the following rhyme, leaving blanks next to the number words. Label 10 index cards with numbers from 1 to 10. Laminate the cards and chart paper for durability. Attach hook-and-loop tape to the chart paper above each blank and to the backs of the cards. Recite the rhyme aloud as a class and have students take turns attaching the correct cards to fill in the blanks on the chart paper.

One, Two, Buckle My Shoe

One _____ , two _____ , buckle my shoe;
Three _____ , four _____ , shut the door;
Five _____ , six _____ , pick up sticks;
Seven _____ , eight _____ , lay them straight;
Nine _____ , ten _____ , a big fat hen.

"Hickory, Dickory, Dock" ⌖ ....

Help students practice telling time to the hour with this familiar rhyme. Make an enlarged copy of the Clock Pattern (page 27) on sturdy paper. Cut out the pieces and laminate them for durability. Use a paper fastener to attach the clock hands to the clock face. Write the following nursery rhyme on a piece of chart paper and display it for the class. Set the clock hands to show a time on the hour. Recite the nursery rhyme aloud as a class and have students fill in the time displayed on the clock when they get to the blank. Change the hour shown on the clock each time the class says the rhyme.

Hickory, Dickory, Dock
Hickory, Dickory, Dock,
The mouse ran up the clock.
The clock struck _____ ;
The mouse ran down,
Hickory, Dickory, Dock.

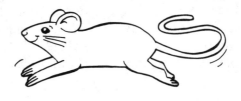

Goose Feathers ABAB ....

Make feather patterns with the class. Give each student a colorful feather (available at most craft stores). (*Caution:* Before completing any feather activity, inquire about students' allergies.) Have six students stand in a line to create a pattern with their feathers. Let the other students recite the following nursery rhyme while the pattern is being assembled.

Cackle, Cackle, Mother Goose
Cackle, cackle, Mother Goose,
Have you any feathers loose?
Truly have I, pretty fellow,
Quite enough to fill a pillow.

Ask the rest of the students to guess the next feather in the pattern. Continue adding students with feathers to the pattern. Challenge students to design more complex patterns for others to continue.

"Cobbler, Cobbler, Mend My Shoe"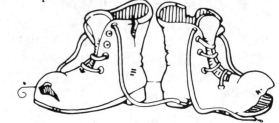

Make a floor-sized graph to compare students' shoes. First, have students sit in a circle on the floor with their feet inside the circle. Talk about the types of shoes everyone is wearing, how they are fastened (laces, buckles, etc.), what they are used for (dress, running, etc.), and colors of shoes (black, brown, etc.). Choose a few types of shoes for the graph's categories. Draw a sample of each type and label it on an index card. Label one index card *other*. Put the index cards in a horizontal line on the floor to create the base of the graph. Recite the following nursery rhyme together as each student takes off one shoe and places it in the appropriate column of the graph. Students whose shoes are not exact matches for the columns should place their shoes in the *other* column. Count aloud how many shoes are in each column and compare the quantities.

> ***Cobbler, Cobbler, Mend My Shoe***
> Cobbler, cobbler, mend my shoe;
> Get it done by half-past two.
> Stitch it up and stitch it down.
> Then, I'll give you half a crown.

"One, Two, Three, Four, Five" (finger play) 1²3

Have students say this catchy chant while performing the movements.

One, Two, Three, Four, Five

One, two, three, four, five,	(Hold up one finger at a time on one hand.)
Once I caught a fish alive;	(Pretend to hold a fishing pole.)
Six, seven, eight, nine, ten,	(Hold up one finger at a time on the other hand.)
But, I let it go again.	(Put hands together and wiggle them like a swimming fish.)
Why did I let it go?	(Raise hands and shrug shoulders.)
Because it bit my finger so!	(Hold up one finger.)
Which finger did it bite?	(Wiggle all 10 fingers.)
The little one on the right.	(Hold up and wave pinky finger on right hand.)

Three Bears Sort ABAB

Read *Goldilocks and the Three Bears* to students and emphasize the concepts of small, medium, and large found in the story. Make enlarged copies of the *Goldilocks and the Three Bears* Cards (page 28). Cut apart the cards and laminate them for durability. Draw three simple house outlines (small, medium, and large) on a piece of poster board. Attach hook-and-loop tape to the backs of the cards and to the fronts of the houses. Let pairs of students take turns sorting the cards by size or type and attaching them to the poster board. Encourage students to use the cards to make patterns for each other to continue, as well.

Clock Pattern

Activity found on page 25.

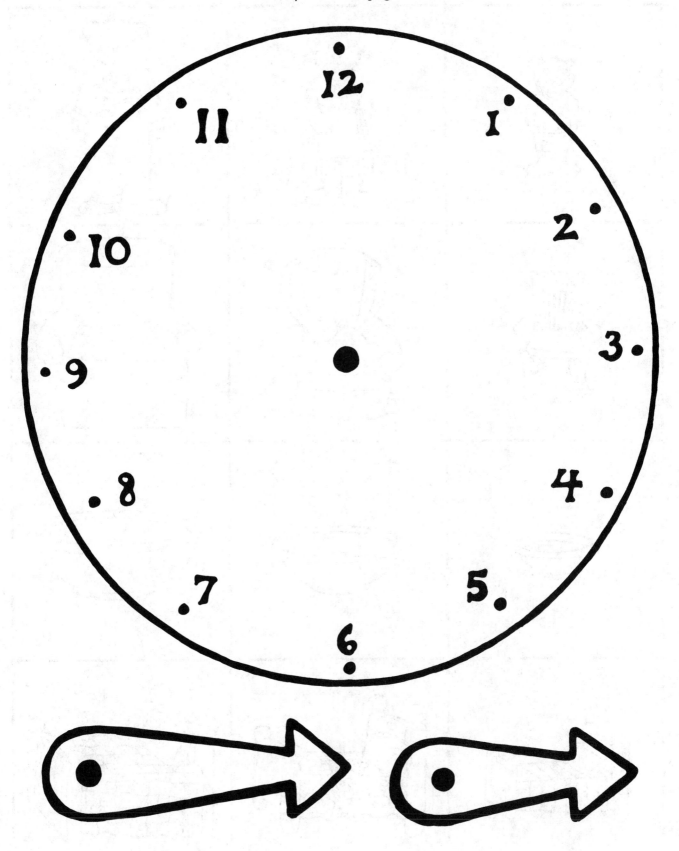

27 CD-104199 *It's Number Time!*

Goldilocks & the Three Bears Cards

Activity found on page 26.

Ocean Animals

Counting Ocean Animals Mini-Book  ....

Help students create counting mini-books. Make an enlarged copy of the Counting Ocean Animals Mini-Book Pattern (page 31) for each student. Then, cut along the dotted lines and staple the pages together to make mini-books. Give each student a mini-book and let her write her name on the cover. Encourage students to color the ocean animals after they count them aloud. Let students take the completed books home to continue counting practice. (If students are able to write numbers from 1 to 5, cover the numbers on the pattern page before making copies. Then, students can write the numbers themselves when they count the ocean animals.)

Swimming Together ABAB ....

Reduce and make several copies of the Ocean Animal Patterns (page 32) on colorful paper. Cut out the animals and glue some of them to sentence strips to create simple patterns (ABAB, AAB, etc.). Laminate the sentence strips and remaining animals for durability. Have students place the ocean animal pieces on the sentence strips to continue the patterns. Encourage students to create new patterns for classmates to continue, as well.

What's in the Ocean? 1²3 ∴ +/- ....

Place a large piece of blue bulletin board paper on the floor to represent an ocean. Make several enlarged copies of the Ocean Animal Patterns (page 32) on colorful paper. Cut out the animals and laminate them for durability. Label index cards with numbers from 1 to 10. Have students sit in a circle around the "ocean" and put the ocean animal pieces in a pile nearby. Place a number card in the "water" and choose a student to count and place the correct number of ocean animals around the number. For a challenge, put a second number card in the water and select another student to count and place the correct number of ocean animals around that number. Have the class complete an addition problem by counting both sets of animals aloud to determine how many animals are in the water.

Ocean Animal Flash Cards +/- ....

Make several copies of the Ocean Animal Patterns (page 32) and cut them out. Glue the animals to large index cards. Write simple addition and subtraction problems on the fronts of the cards and write the answers on the backs. Laminate the cards for durability. Let students practice addition skills by solving the problems and checking their answers. Students can complete this activity alone or with partners.

Sea Life Sorting ΑΒΑΒ

Choose several colors of paper and make two copies of the Ocean Animal Patterns (page 32) on each color. Repeat the process with a reduced set of copies and an enlarged set of copies. Cut out the animals and laminate for durability. Have students sort the animals by species, color, or size. If desired, challenge students to time themselves to see how quickly they can sort the cutouts. Then, let them try to beat their own best times. The cutouts can also be used for patterning activities.

Schools of Fish ∴ 1²3 ⊡2

Encourage students' creativity by having them decorate schools of unique fish. Enlarge and copy the fish from the Ocean Animal Patterns (page 32) for each student. Provide art materials, such as markers, crayons, fabric pieces, and pieces of yarn or ribbon, for students to use to decorate the fish. Have students cut out the decorated fish and help them post the fish in schools on a bulletin board. Include a different number of fish in each school. On additional Ocean Animal Patterns, write a matching number for each school of fish. Let students count the fish in each school and then attach the correctly numbered ocean animal beside each school.

Under the Sea 1²3 ∴ ◎◎

Make an activity board by gluing or drawing an underwater scene on a piece of poster board. Laminate the activity board for durability. Make two sets of the Ocean Animal Patterns (page 32). Then, reduce and copy 15 sets of the ocean animals. Cut out and laminate all of the pieces for durability. Using a write-on/wipe-away marker, label the regular-size cutouts with numbers from 1 to 8. Sort the small cutouts by types of animals. To play the game, a student should choose one of the numbered cutouts, read the number, and then place the corresponding number of small animal cutouts in a group on the activity board to make an ocean scene. For example, if a student chooses a jellyfish cutout with a number 5 written on it, he should place five small jellyfish cutouts together on the activity board. Play continues until the ocean is full of animals. Occasionally, wipe off the numbers and reprogram the cutouts to change the ocean scene.

Counting Ocean Animals Mini-Book Pattern

Activity found on page 29.

2 turtles

5 starfish

1 octopus

4 fish

I Can Count to 5!

Name:

3 dolphins

CD-104199 *It's Number Time!*

Ocean Animal Patterns

Activities found on pages 29–30.

Pets

Good Dog!

Make 10 enlarged copies of the Dog Pattern (page 36) and cut them out. Glue the patterns to paper plates to make "dog dishes." Make 20 copies of the Dog Bone Pattern (page 36) on brown paper. Program half of the bones with numbers from 1 to 10 and the other half with sets from 1 to 10. Code the backs of the matching bones with colorful stickers or markings for self-checking. Laminate the bones for durability. To play, have students spread the 10 dog dishes on the floor. Then, students should sort the dog bones so that each dog has a matching pair of bones. When finished, students can turn over all of the bones to check their work.

Where Has My Little Dog Gone?

Make 22 enlarged copies of the Dog Pattern (page 36) on colorful paper. Cut out the patterns and program them with two sets of numbers from 0 to 10. Laminate the cutouts for durability. Punch a hole at the top of each pattern and thread a piece of yarn through each one. Tie the ends of the yarn together to create necklaces. Give each student a necklace to wear. Have students scatter around the room and then begin looking for classmates with matching numbers on their necklaces. When students find their matches, tell them to stand together until everyone has found a match.

Finding Felines

Make 22 enlarged copies of the Cat Pattern (page 36) on colorful paper. Cut out the patterns and program 11 cats with numbers from 0 to 10. Program the remaining cats with sets from 0 to 10. Laminate the cats for durability. To play, have students sit in a circle on the floor. Give each student a cat cutout. Have one student hold up his cat cutout, then have the student with the match hold up her cat cutout. Let the whole class call out the number represented on the matching cutouts. Continue play until all of the cutouts have been matched.

Say Cheese! 1st

Cut out 11 cheese wedge shapes from yellow paper. Using a black marker, draw a number of holes (circles) to make sets from 0 to 10 on each cheese wedge. Laminate the cheese wedges for durability. To play, have students count the number of holes on each cheese wedge and then place the patterns in order from the largest number of holes to the smallest number or from smallest number to largest number. Students can also randomly select two cheese wedge patterns and compare them to determine which has more holes and which has fewer holes.

Bunny Hop 1²3

Using masking tape, make several large shapes on the floor, such as a square, triangle, and rectangle. Divide students into groups and have each group stand around a shape. Call out a shape and a number. The students standing around that shape should then "bunny hop" in and out of the shape the corresponding number of times. For example, if you say, "Square, five," students around the square should jump in and out of the square five times while the entire class counts aloud.

Frogs & More Frogs 1²3

Spread a piece of bulletin board paper on a table or on the floor. Make 10 copies of the Lily Pad Pattern (page 37) on green paper. Cut out the patterns and number them from 1 to 10. Then, attach the lily pads in random order in a column on the left side of the bulletin board paper. Make 55 copies of the Frog Pattern (page 37) on colorful paper and cut them out. Have students take turns choosing a lily pad, counting the corresponding number of frogs, and placing the frogs in a row beside the lily pad. When all of the rows are complete, have students compare their rows to determine which have more frogs and which have fewer frogs.

Five Speckled Frogs 1st +/−

Make a frog finger puppet for yourself and one for each student. Reduce and copy the Frog Pattern (page 37) on green paper. Cut out the patterns and attach each to a ring of card stock that is sized to fit around the wearer's finger. Wear the finger puppets as you recite the following rhyme with students. The rhyme traditionally starts with five frogs; if desired, start the rhyme with 10 frogs.

Five Speckled Frogs

Five speckled frogs sitting on a log,   (Hold up five fingers.)
Eating some delicious bugs.
Yum! Yum!   (Pat stomach.)

One frog jumped in the pool,   (Hold up the puppet and then hide it behind your back.)
Where it was nice and cool,
Now there are four speckled frogs.   (Hold up four fingers.)
Glub! Glub!

Continue with:
"Four speckled frogs sitting on a log," etc., until there are no frogs left.

Swim, Fishy, Swim!

Cut out a large pond shape from blue bulletin board paper. Use a marker to draw familiar shapes (circle, square, triangle, etc.) around the edge of the pond. Instruct a student to "swim" (walk while moving her arms and body as if she is a swimming fish) around the edge of the pond, stepping on one shape at a time. As she steps on a shape, the student should name it before moving on. For a challenge, have students also name an object that is the shape before moving on.

Pop-Up Puppets

Make one copy of the Bird Pattern (page 38) on colorful paper for each student. Program each bird with a number. (If students only know numbers through 10 and there are more than 10 students in the class, make two sets of birds numbered from 1 to 10.) Cut out the birds and laminate them for durability. Glue each bird to a craft stick to make a puppet. Cut the bottom out of a cylindrical oatmeal box. Wrap the resulting tube in paper. Have one student insert a puppet into the tube to hide it, being careful not to let others see it. At your signal, have the student slide the tube down her arm to pop the bird up and allow classmates to see its number. The first student to name the number correctly gets to hide the next puppet in the tube. Continue playing until all of the students have had a turn.

Birds on a Wire 1st

Enlarge and make 11 copies of the Bird Pattern (page 38) on colorful paper. Program the birds with numbers from 0 to 10. Cut out the birds and laminate them for durability. Attach a piece of yarn or string across a bulletin board at students' eye level. Using clothespins or paper clips, have students attach the birds to the yarn in numerical order. For a challenge, have students arrange the birds in reverse numerical order.

Leaping Lizards 1st

Attach a piece of masking tape to the floor in a straight line extending several feet. Make 11 enlarged copies of the Lizard Pattern (page 38) and program each with a number from 0 to 10. Cut out the lizards and laminate them for durability. Attach the lizards sequentially at even intervals along the tape line. For added stability, cover each pattern with a piece of clear contact paper. To use the number line, have students take turns scurrying like lizards from one number to the next, naming each number as they land on it. For added fun, play or sing a counting song and have students take turns leaping to each number as it is named in the song.

Our Favorite Pets 1²3

Draw a blank graph with an x-axis and a y-axis on a piece of bulletin board paper. Place the graph on a table or hang it low on a wall or bulletin board where students can reach it. Give each student a large index card and have him draw a picture of his favorite kind of pet. (He does not necessarily need to own the pet.) Students can also cut out pictures of pets from magazines and glue them to their index cards. Help students label their cards with the names of the types of pets. When students' cards are complete, have them tape the cards in columns on the graph according to the types of pets. Then, have students count aloud the number of pets in each column to decide which pet is the most popular.

Dog Bone, Dog, & Cat Patterns

Activities found on page 33.

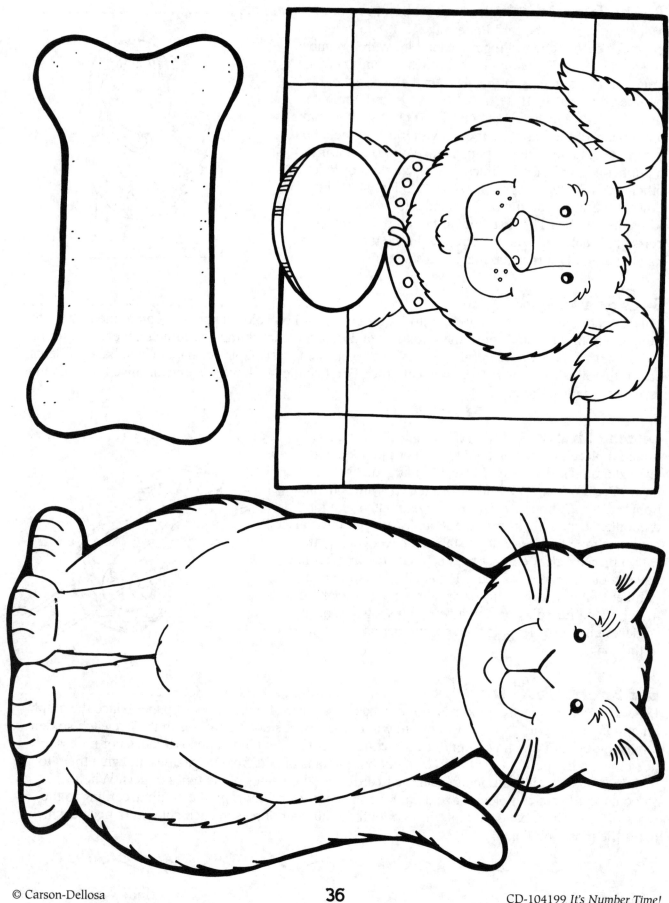

36

CD-104199 *It's Number Time!*

Frog & Lily Pad Patterns

Activities found on page 34.

Bird & Lizard Patterns

Activities found on page 35.

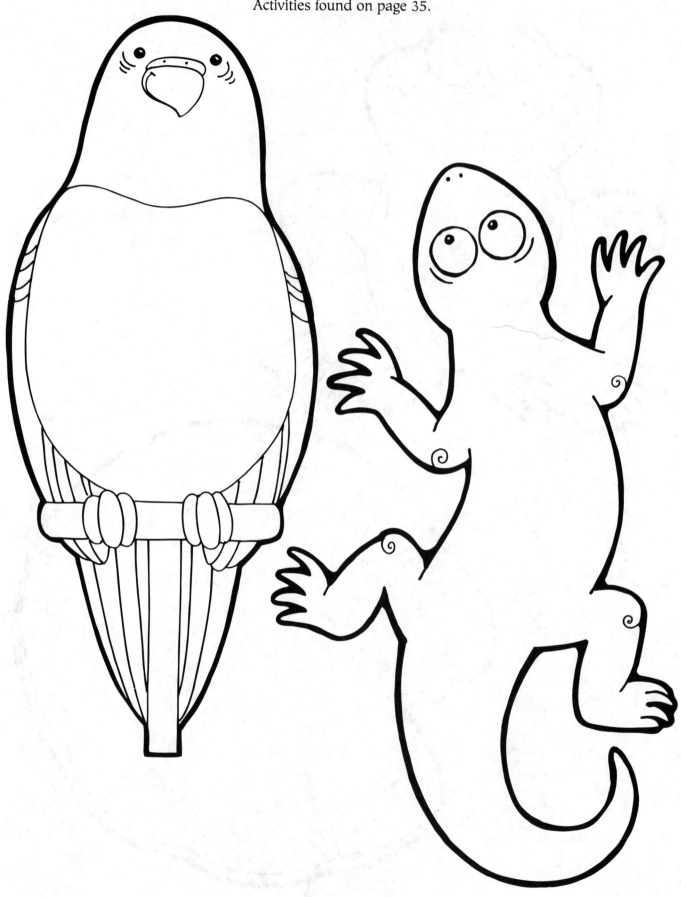

Seasons: Fall

Let's Go Apple Picking

Make 11 copies each of the Apple and Leaf Patterns (page 41) on red and green paper. Cut out the pieces. Program each leaf with a number and each apple with a number set for numbers from 0 to 10. Laminate the apples and leaves for durability. Play the game as a class by giving each student a leaf or an apple. Have students walk around and find classmates with the matching pieces.

An Appealing Graph

Make a graph to determine which kind of apple is the class's favorite. Draw a graph with three columns on a paper-covered bulletin board. Make several copies of the Apple Patterns (page 41) on red, green, and yellow paper. Cut out the patterns and place them near the graph. Bring red, green, and yellow apple slices for students to sample and let each student decide which type of apple is his favorite. Let him choose an apple pattern that matches his preference, write his name on the pattern, and attach it in the appropriate column on the graph. Have students count aloud to determine how many students like each type of apple.

Apple Bingo

Reinforce number recognition by playing bingo with students. Make a game board by drawing a grid five squares wide by six squares high. Write the letters of the word *bingo* in the squares of the top row and mark the center square *free*. Make a copy of the game board for each student. Program the game boards randomly with numbers from 0 to 20 (or from 0 to 10 if students are not familiar with numbers through 20). Create caller's cards by numbering a set of index cards from 0 to 20 (or 10). Give each student a game board and a small, resealable plastic bag of space markers, such as apple-flavored cereal or small apple cutouts. To play, hold up a caller's card and read the number aloud. If a student has that number on her game board, she should cover the number with a marker in each square where it appears. Play continues until a student covers all of the squares on her board and calls out, "Bingo!" Or, for a faster game, have students call out, "Bingo!" when they cover all of the numbers in one row.

Five Little Apples (finger play)

Have students say the following chant while performing the movements.

Five Little Apples

Five little apples sitting on the floor;	*(Hold up five fingers.)*
One rolls away, and then there are four.	*(Move hands in a rolling motion.)*
Four little apples sitting in a tree;	*(Hold up four fingers.)*
You pick one, and then there are three.	*(Pretend to reach up to pick an apple.)*
Three little apples, what should we do?	*(Hold up three fingers.)*
Put one your basket, and then there are two.	*(Pretend to put an apple in a basket.)*
Two little apples sitting in the sun;	*(Hold up two fingers.)*
Pick one up, and then there is one.	*(Pretend to reach down to pick up an apple.)*
One little apple left from the bunch;	*(Hold up one finger.)*
I'll eat it up with a loud CRUNCH, CRUNCH!	*(Pretend to take a bite of an apple.)*

Silly Jack-O'-Lanterns ABAB ⚭

Make four copies of the Pumpkin Patterns (page 42) on white paper. Use a black marker to draw a different silly face on each of the four pumpkins. Then, copy them onto orange paper. Reduce the patterns and make a set of smaller copies. Reduce the patterns again to make a set of even smaller pumpkins. Cut out all of the pumpkins and laminate them for durability. Place the pumpkins in a plastic pumpkin bucket. To play, have pairs of students sort the pumpkins by size or facial features. Students can also make patterns or sequence the pumpkins by size.

Fall Counting Mural ◠◠ 1²3

Cover a large table with bulletin board paper and draw a simple scarecrow, several haystacks, and a large apple tree. Use markers or paint to color the objects. On several index cards, draw a simple picture of either a pumpkin, an apple, or a crow. Beside each picture, write a number from 1 to 5. Place the cards in a container near the mural. Have each student choose a card and then draw and color the number of pumpkins, apples, or crows somewhere on the mural. When each student has contributed to the mural, count the pumpkins, apples, and crows together. Hang the mural on a wall or bulletin board for a fall decoration.

Puzzling Pumpkin Problems +/- ∴ ⚂

Make several copies of the Pumpkin Patterns (page 42) on orange paper. On the bottom half of each pumpkin, write a simple addition or subtraction problem. On the top half, use pumpkin stickers or stamps to show the sum or difference for the problem. Cut the pumpkins in half to create two puzzle pieces. Be sure to cut the puzzles unevenly so that as students fit the pieces together, each piece only fits with its correctly matching piece. Laminate the pieces for durability. To play, have students look at each problem and find the sum or difference to complete each puzzle.

Pumpkin Picassos ✐

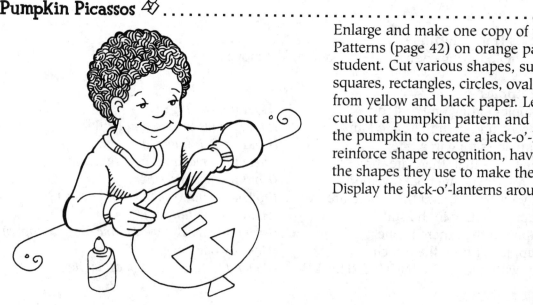

Enlarge and make one copy of the Pumpkin Patterns (page 42) on orange paper for each student. Cut various shapes, such as triangles, squares, rectangles, circles, ovals, and semicircles, from yellow and black paper. Let each student cut out a pumpkin pattern and glue shapes onto the pumpkin to create a jack-o'-lantern. To reinforce shape recognition, have students name the shapes they use to make their silly faces. Display the jack-o'-lanterns around the classroom.

Apple & Leaf Patterns

Activities found on page 39.

CD-104199 *It's Number Time!*

Pumpkin Patterns

Activities found on page 40.

CD-104199 *It's Number Time!*

Seasons: Winter

How Many Snowballs? 1²3 ⊙⊙

How many snowballs does it take to make a snowman? Give each student a copy of the Snowman Pattern (page 45), glue, and cotton balls. Have each student guess how many cotton balls she thinks it will take to cover the snowman. Help each student write the number on her snowman's hat. Then, let students glue cotton balls to the snowmen. When they are finished, have students count how many cotton balls they used and compare the totals to their estimates. (If desired, have students count the cotton balls as they work instead of counting when they are finished gluing.) Depending on students' counting skills, you may want to make reduced copies of the Snowman Pattern so that each student will not need as many cotton balls to complete the activity. Or, have students count how many cotton balls it takes to complete the perimeter of the snowman.

Collecting Snowballs ⚁ 1²3 ⸪ ◌◌ ⊙⊙

Explain that students should wear mittens when they play outside in the snow, especially when they make snowballs. To play this game, pairs of students will collect "snowballs" to match to the mittens. Copy the Mitten Patterns (page 46) on colorful paper. Program each mitten with a number from 0 to 10. Laminate the mittens for durability. Provide cotton balls or white craft pom-poms to represent snowballs. Have each player choose a mitten, read the number written on it, and collect a matching set of "snowballs." Then, have students compare their sets to determine who has more and who has fewer.

Where Are My Mittens? ⚁

Copy and cut out eight reduced pairs of Mitten Patterns (page 46). Decorate each pair of mittens with a unique pattern. Attach the left mittens in random order along the top of an open file folder and attach the right mittens along the bottom. Punch a hole directly below each mitten. Cut eight pieces of colorful yarn and thread each one through the hole below a left mitten cutout. Tape the yarn to the back of the folder to secure it in place. To play the game, a student should find a match and thread the left mitten's piece of yarn to the matching right mitten, continuing until all of the pieces have been matched. Make the game self-checking by circling each right mitten hole on the back of the folder in the same color as the correct piece of yarn.

All Buttoned Up! 1st 123

Make 11 copies of the Snowman Pattern (page 45) and program each snowman's hat with a number from 0 to 10. Cut out the snowmen and laminate them for durability. Place a container of buttons and the snowmen at a learning center. To play the game, have students read the numbers on the snowmen and put them in sequential order. Then, students should count the matching number of buttons for each snowman and place them on the patterns.

Match Those Mittens

Copy a pair of Mitten Patterns (page 46) for each student to decorate and cut out. Instruct students to color both of their mittens the same way so that they match. Collect all of the left mittens in one pile and spread all of the right mittens on the floor. Have students sit in a circle around the mittens. Give each student a left mitten. Let students take turns finding the matching mittens. This game can also be played in pairs or small groups at a center.

Warming Up with Patterns ABAB 1st

Let students use mittens to practice patterning. Copy several of the Mitten Patterns (page 46) in three sizes on different colors of paper and cut them out. Laminate the cutouts for durability. Begin a color pattern, such as blue, white, blue, white; or a size pattern, such as large, small, large, small. Then, have students continue the pattern. Allow students to design additional pattern activities for classmates to complete. If desired, number the mittens before laminating and let students use the cutouts for sequencing practice, as well.

The Most Snowballs

Make "snowballs" by cutting out 22 circles from white paper. Divide the circles into two groups of 11 and program each with a number from 0 to 10. Store each set of circles in a resealable plastic bag. To play, each student in a pair opens a bag, shuffles the snowballs, and stacks them facedown in front of him. Each player should then draw a snowball from his stack and turn it over. The player with the largest number showing takes both snowballs and places them facedown at the bottom of his pile. If the numbers match, the first player to say, "Snowball!" takes both snowballs. Play continues until one player has won all of the snowballs.

Snowman Pattern

Activities found on pages 43–44.

Mitten Patterns

Activities found on pages 43–44.

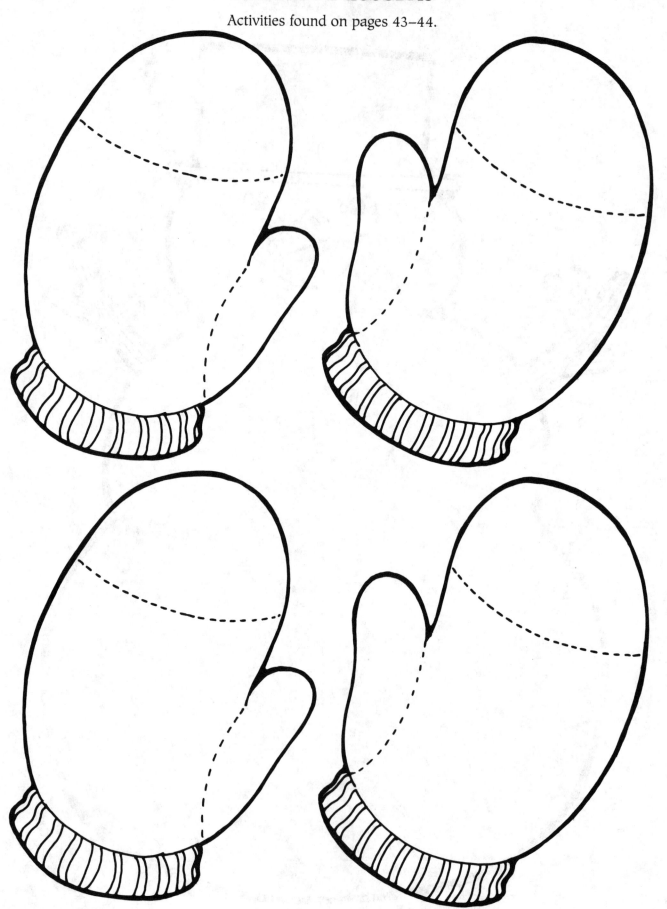

Seasons: Spring

Fabulous Flower Matching

Make 11 copies of the Flower, Stem, and Flowerpot Patterns (page 49) on colorful paper. Cut out the pieces and glue the flowers to the stems. Program each flower with a number from 0 to 10 and program each flowerpot with a number set from 0 to 10. Laminate the pieces for durability. Give each student a flower or a flowerpot. Have students stand or sit in a large circle. Choose a student with a flowerpot pattern and have him place it on the floor in the middle of the circle. Ask the student with the matching flower to "plant" it in the flowerpot. Continue playing until all of the flowers have been "planted." Then, pick up the pieces and redistribute them. Students who had flowers in the first round should have flowerpots in the second round so that all of the students have a chance to plant flowers.

Flower Rainbow Booklets

Help students make counting rainbow books. First, make six templates on white copy paper. Along the bottom edge of each piece of paper, write one of the following phrases: _____ *red flower,* _____ *orange flowers,* _____ *yellow flowers,* _____ *green flowers,* _____ *blue flowers,* _____ *purple flowers.* Make one copy of each template on the corresponding color paper for each student. Stack the six pieces vertically in rainbow order for each student with a sheet of white paper on top and the purple paper on the bottom. Beginning with the blue paper, cut the top edge of each piece of paper so that it is 1" (2.5 cm) shorter than the piece behind it. When stacking the pieces of paper in order again, align them at the top so that the white paper is the shortest, and the purple paper is the longest, with a rainbow of colors showing in between. Staple the pages along the top to make a book that shows the text at the bottom of the pages. (See illustration.) Have students write a number from 1 to 6 to fill in the blank on each colorful page. Then, on the white sheets of paper, have students draw colorful bouquets of flowers and write their names. Finally, let students use stamps, stickers, markers, or crayons to add the matching number of flowers in the appropriate color on each page.

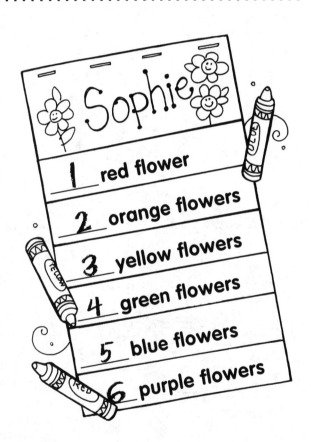

Potting Plants

Collect 10 sturdy, plastic flowerpots. Cut a plastic foam circle to fit securely inside each flowerpot. Label each flowerpot with a number from 1 to 10. Provide two pairs of child-sized gardening gloves, two gardening hats, two aprons, and 55 artificial flowers (available at most craft stores). To play, have a pair of students wear the hats, aprons, and gloves and "plant" the correct number of flowers in each flowerpot by pushing the stems into the plastic foam. Encourage students to count aloud as they plant the flowers.

Counting Flower "Seeds" 1²3 ∴ 👀 ✏️

Make 10 enlarged copies of the Flower Pattern (page 49) on yellow paper. On each pattern, write a number from 1 to 10 for students to trace. (If desired, write the numbers with dotted lines.) Cut out and laminate the patterns for durability. Supply students with a container of large dried beans to represent flower seeds. Let students use write-on/wipe-away markers to trace each number and then count the matching number of seeds to put on the flower.

Flower Power Math +/- 🎲

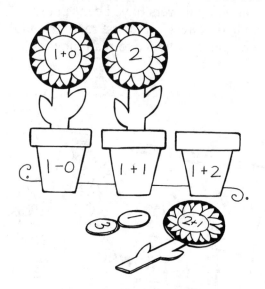

Make several copies of the Flower, Stem, and Flowerpot Patterns (page 49) on colorful paper. Cut out the pieces. Glue the flowers to the stems and program each flower with a simple addition or subtraction problem. Program each flowerpot with another simple addition or subtraction problem that has the same answer as a problem written on a flower. Cut out light brown circles the same size as the center of a flower and program them with the sums or differences for the problems. Laminate the pieces for durability. To play, have each student choose a flower, read the problem, and match it to a flowerpot with a problem that has the same answer. Then, the student should find the circle with the sum or difference for the problems shown on the flower and flowerpot.

Growth Spurts ⭕⭕ ② 1²3

Provide two small flowerpots (or paper cups) for each student. Allow students to decorate their flowerpots and write their names on them. Then, help students plant flower seeds or small seedlings that grow quickly. Place half of the flowerpots on a sunny windowsill and half in a shady area. Encourage students to keep the soil moist and monitor the plants' growth. As the flowers grow, have students compare the seedlings to determine which ones are growing faster. Keep track of the progress by marking on a calendar when leaves, buds, and blooms appear. Review the calendar with students and have them count the number of days it took for each part of the plant to appear.

Gauging Spring 📊 ✏️ ⭕⭕

Collect a small plastic bottle (disposable drink bottles work well) for each student. Cut the necks off the bottles. Then, use a permanent marker to mark ½" and 1" (1.25 cm and 2.5 cm) increments on the bottles to create rain gauges. Ask students to have their families help them use the gauges to measure rain amounts at their houses and then bring the data to class to compare results. Display the results on a graph. Over time, ask the class who had the most rain at her house and who had the least.

Flower, Stem, & Flowerpot Patterns

Activities found on pages 47–48.

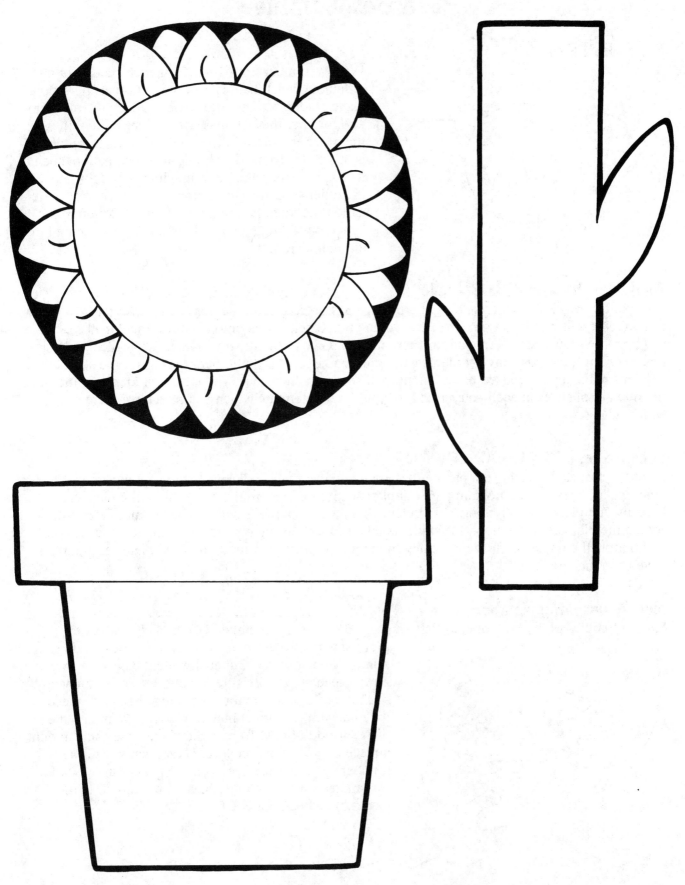

Seasons: Summer

Beach Ball Fun

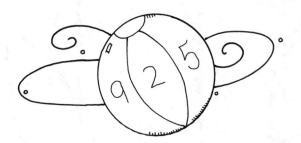

Write a number from 1 to 10 on each section of an inflatable beach ball. Or, draw a set on each section. Have students stand in a circle. Call a student's name and toss her the ball. Ask the student to identify the number written in the section her right thumb is touching. Then, she should name an action, such as clapping, hopping, or doing jumping jacks. Have the other students count aloud as they complete the action the identified number of times. Continue the beach ball fun by having the student toss the ball to another classmate.

Seed Search

Make one copy of the Watermelon Pattern (page 52) on colorful paper for each student. Make "seed" sets to represent numbers from 1 to 5 by gluing dried black beans onto each watermelon slice. There will be more than one watermelon for each number. Give each student a watermelon slice and ask him to count the seeds. Have students write their names and the number of seeds on the slices. Help students make a graph based on the number of seeds on each slice. Then, have students count aloud the number of slices in each column of the graph and determine which columns have more and which have fewer.

Let's Go on a Picnic

Create picnic sets by cutting out pictures of food from magazines and gluing them in groups from 1 to 10 onto paper plates. Then, program paper napkins with numbers from 1 to 10. Store the plates and napkins in a picnic basket along with a picnic blanket. To play the game, have a pair of students spread the blanket on the floor. Let students take turns choosing a plate, counting the pictures on it, and finding the napkin with the matching number. Continue play until all of the plates and napkins have been matched.

Mouth-Watering Numbers

Make 11 copies of the Watermelon Pattern (page 52) on colorful paper. Use a black marker to program each watermelon slice with a corresponding number and seed set. Cut each watermelon slice to make a two-piece puzzle. Be sure to cut the puzzles unevenly so that as students fits the pieces together, each piece only fits with its correct matching piece. Laminate the pieces for durability. To play the game, give each student a piece of a watermelon slice. Let students read the numbers or count the seeds on their slices and look for classmates with matching slices. Play until all of the pieces have been matched.

Scrumptious Scoops 👀 ∴ 1²3 ....

Make 11 copies of the Ice Cream Cone Patterns (page 53) on light brown paper. Program each cone with a number from 0 to 10. Copy 55 Scoop of Ice Cream Patterns (page 53) on colorful paper. Cut out the cones and scoops and laminate them for durability. Have pairs of students take turns choosing an ice cream cone and placing the matching number of scoops on top.

Making Sundaes 👀 ∴ 1²3 ....

Program the insides of 10 paper bowls with numbers from 1 to 10. Provide "scoops of ice cream" by gathering 55 large, colorful craft pom-poms or painting small, plastic foam balls in a variety of colors. Place the scoops of ice cream in a clean, empty ice cream container and provide an ice cream scoop. Have students sit in a circle on the floor. Pass out the bowls. (Make sure the bowls with higher numbers are large enough to hold that number of scoops of ice cream.) Then, pass the container and scoop around the circle and let students take turns placing the matching number of scoops of ice cream in the bowls. Have the class count aloud as students scoop the ice cream. Continue playing until each student has had a turn to scoop ice cream into a bowl.

More Ice Cream, Please! ∴ 1²3 ⊕ ....

Copy two Ice Cream Cone Patterns (page 53) on light brown paper. Copy 110 Scoop of Ice Cream Patterns (page 53) on colorful paper. Cut out the patterns and laminate for durability. Program 22 index cards with sets from 0 to 10. Give each player an ice cream cone. Have students shuffle and place the index cards facedown in a stack. Each student should take a turn choosing a card and placing the correct number of scoops of ice cream on his cone. Then, have students compare their sets and decide who has more scoops. The player with more scoops keeps all of the scoops. If the number of scoops is the same, each player keeps his own. Let students continue playing until all of the cards have been selected. The student with the most scoops of ice cream at the end of the game is the winner.

Tasty Toppings 👀 ∴ 1²3 ....

Make an enlarged copy of the Counting Sprinkles Mini-Book Pattern (page 54) for each student. Then, cut along the dotted lines and staple the pages together to make mini-books. Give each student a mini-book and let her write her name on the cover. Have students read the number at the bottom of each page and then use crayons or markers to draw the matching number of sprinkles on each ice cream cone or sundae. Encourage students to color the cones and sundaes after they draw the sprinkles. Let students take the completed books home to continue counting practice. (If students are able to write numbers from 6 to 10, cover the numbers on the pattern page before making copies. Then, students can write the numbers themselves before they draw the sprinkles. For this option, dictate to students which numbers to fill in or provide sets for them to count and write the corresponding numbers.)

Watermelon Pattern

Activities found on page 50.

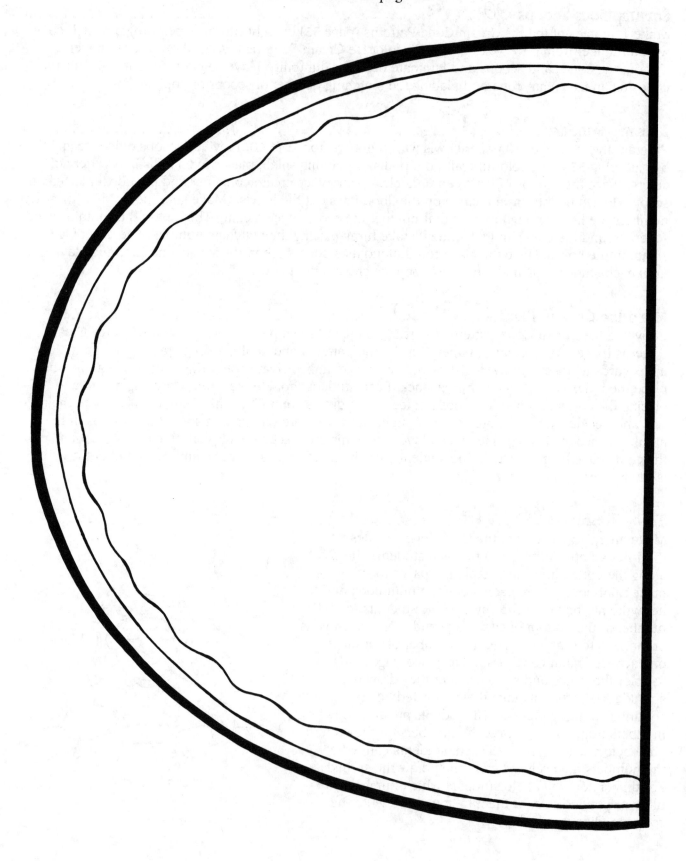

Ice Cream Cone & Scoop of Ice Cream Patterns

Activities found on page 51.

53 CD-104199 *It's Number Time!*

Counting Sprinkles Mini-Book Pattern

Activity found on page 51.

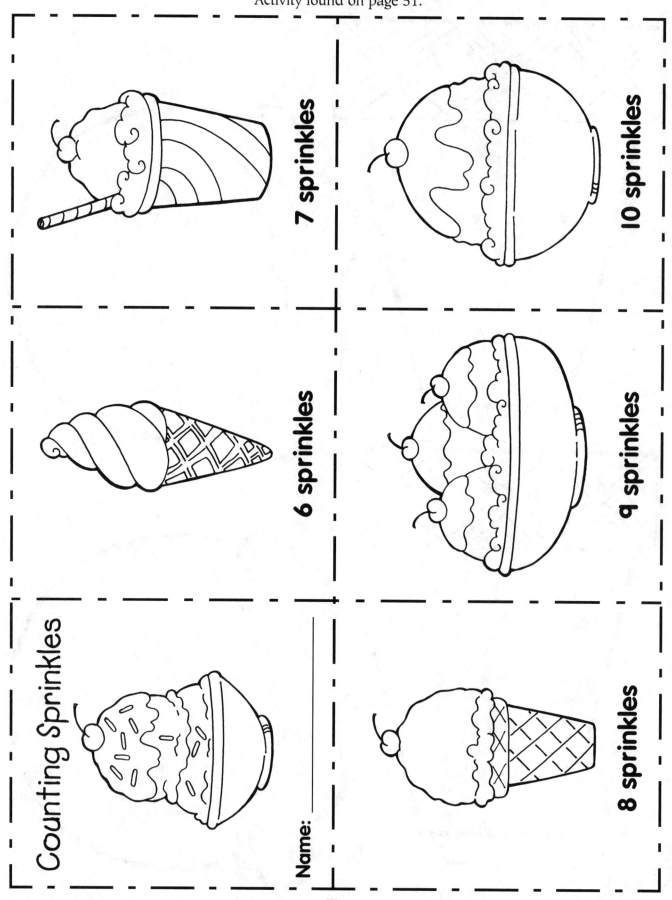

7 sprinkles

10 sprinkles

6 sprinkles

9 sprinkles

Counting Sprinkles

Name:

8 sprinkles

CD-104199 *It's Number Time!*

Space

Flying through the Stars ∴ 1²3 . . . .
For each player, prepare a sentence strip with 20 colorful star stickers or stamps in a row. Make 20 reduced copies of the Spaceship Pattern (page 56) on colorful paper for each player. Cut out and laminate the spaceships for durability. To play, one student rolls a fair number cube and counts the matching number of spaceships aloud, placing each spaceship on top of a star on her sentence strip. Players take turns rolling the cube and counting spaceships until each player has covered all of the stars on her sentence strip.

Star-Studded Numbers ◷◷ 1²3 ∴ ✏ . . . .
Create number worksheets for students using copy paper. Turn a piece of paper horizontally. On the left half of the paper, draw a large outline of a number from 1 to 10. Leave the right half of the paper blank. Make a template for each number from 1 to 10 and make a copy of each worksheet for each student. Place the worksheets at a center with ink pads, markers, and star stamps. Each student should choose a number worksheet, use a star stamp to decorate the inside of the number outline, and then use a marker to write the number in the blank space on the right side of the paper. Across the bottom of the page, the student should stamp a row of stars equal to the number written on the worksheet. Students can repeat this process to complete several different worksheets at a time, depending on the focus of the lesson.

Fly to the Moon ◷◷ 1st . . . .
For each player, make 11 copies each of the Star and Spaceship Patterns (page 56) and one copy of the Moon Pattern (page 56) on colorful paper. Cut out the patterns. Attach each set of 11 stars and a moon to a sentence strip. Program the sets of spaceships with numbers from 0 to 10. Laminate the sentence strips and spaceship pieces for durability. To complete the activity, have students shuffle the spaceship pieces and then put them in numerical order on top of the stars on their sentence strips. For a challenge, have students put the spaceships in reverse numerical order.

Starry Night ◷◷ ∴ 🎲 . . . .
Make 22 enlarged copies of the Star Pattern (page 56) on colorful paper. Cut out the stars. On 11 stars, write a number from 0 to 10 and glue them randomly to a piece of poster board. Draw a space scene around the stars. Program the remaining 11 stars with sets from 0 to 10. Laminate the game board and star cutouts for durability. Give each student a star cutout. Place the game board on the floor and have students match the sets on the stars to the numbers shown on the game board.

Star, Moon, & Spaceship Patterns

Activities found on page 55.

56

CD-104199 *It's Number Time!*

Transportation

All Aboard for Shape Fun

Prepare a supply of shape templates (rectangles, squares, circles, triangles, etc.) in a variety of sizes. Provide colorful paper, pencils, and scissors for students to trace and cut out shapes. Make an enlarged copy of the Train Engine Pattern (page 59) for each shape. Cut out and label each engine with a drawing of a shape. Laminate the engines for durability and post them on a bulletin board. Enlarge and make one copy of the Train Car Pattern (page 59) for each student and cut them out. Let each student choose a shape, trace and cut it out, and glue it to a train car. Then, have students post their cars behind the correct engines to make shape trains.

Number Trains

Make 10 enlarged copies of the Train Engine Pattern (page 59) on colorful paper and cut out the patterns. Label each engine with a number from 1 to 10. Laminate for durability. Enlarge and make 10 copies of the Train Car Pattern (page 59) for each student. Post a numbered train engine on a bulletin board. Give each student a train car to cut out. Then, provide stickers, stamps and ink pads, or markers and have students create sets to match the number shown on the train engine. As students complete their train cars, let them attach the cars to the engine to create a number train. Create more number trains with the remaining engines.

Take Your Seats

Create a classroom bus station, complete with a driver and tickets. Make a row of chairs equal to the number of students in the class. Label the chairs in sequential order by attaching numbered pieces of paper to the backs of the chairs. (If students only know numbers from 1 to 10 and there are more than 10 students in the class, divide the chairs into two rows and label two sets of chairs from 1 to 10.) Pretend to be a bus driver and give each student a "bus ticket" (a slip of paper with a number written on it). To board the bus, students should line up and hand you their tickets. Use a hole punch to "check in" each "passenger" and let him find his seat on the train by matching the number on his ticket to the number on a chair. After all of the students have found their seats, have them count off by reading aloud the numbers on their tickets.

Parade of Cars 🖉 **1**ˢᵗ

Enlarge and make one copy of the Car Pattern (page 59) on colorful paper for each student. Give each student a pattern to cut out. Assign each student a number and let her write it on her car. Help students as needed. (If students only know numbers from 1 to 10 and there are more than 10 students in the class, divide the class into two groups and let each group make numbered cars from 1 to 10.) Have students sit in a large circle and slowly count aloud together. As each number is called, the student (or students) with that number written on her car should add it to a line of cars in the middle of the circle. By the time students have counted to 10, the class will have created a parade of cars in numerical order.

Up, Up, & Away! ABAB

Enlarge and make a supply of the Hot Air Balloon Pattern (page 60) on colorful patterned paper or a variety of solid-colored paper. Cut out the balloons and laminate them for durability. Attach a piece of yarn or string across a bulletin board at students' eye level. Using clothespins or paper clips, attach three or four balloons to the yarn in a pattern. Let students finish the pattern. Students can also create patterns for each other.

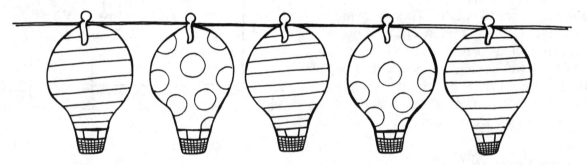

Transportation Identification ABAB

Gather a variety of transportation toys, such as trucks, cars, boats, airplanes, construction vehicles, and community service vehicles. If toys are not readily available, find pictures of modes of transportation in magazines, cut them out, and glue them to index cards. Laminate the cards for durability. Have students sort the modes of transportation in a variety of ways, such as whether the vehicles travel by land, sea, or air; how they are used (for rescue, for construction, taking people to work, etc.); by size; or by the number of passengers they hold.

Sailing into Math ⁺/⁻ 🎲

Create a math problem matching game for students to practice math facts. Copy a supply of the Sailboat Pattern (page 60) on colorful paper. Write addition and subtraction facts on some of the sailboats. Write the answers to the facts on the remaining sailboats. Cut out and laminate the sailboats for durability. Let students match the problems with the correct answers. Students can work with partners or complete this activity independently.

Train Engine, Train Car, & Car Patterns

Activities found on pages 57–58.

Hot Air Balloon & Sailboat Patterns

Activities found on page 58.

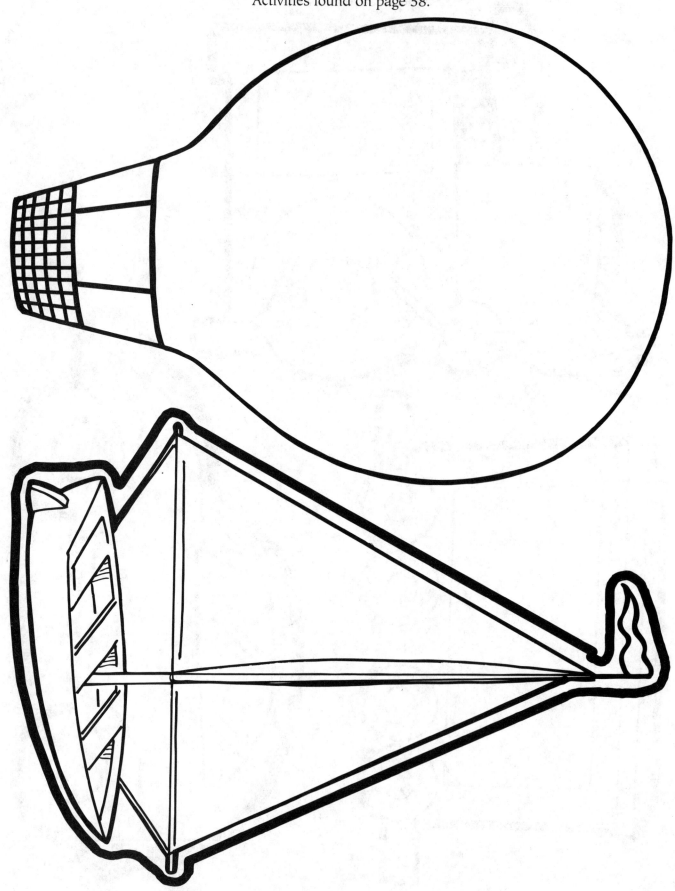

Treats

Cookie Problems ∴ 1²3 ⃝⃝

Make 12 cookie cutouts by copying the Cookie Patterns (page 63) on colorful paper. Cut out and laminate the cookies for durability. Read *The Doorbell Rang* by Pat Hutchins (HarperTrophy, 1989) to students and then use this activity to encourage problem solving. Place the 12 cookie cutouts on a plate and show them to the class. Choose two students and give each one a paper plate. Have the class help divide the cookies evenly between the two students' plates. Then, ring a bell to represent a doorbell and invite two more students to take plates. Have the class help divide the cookies evenly between the four students. Continue in this manner until there are 12 students, each with one cookie on her plate. Ring the doorbell once more and ask the class how the cookies should be shared when the final "visitor" arrives. If desired, read the story aloud again and talk about the surprise ending.

Sweet Treats ABAB 1²3 ⅲ ✏

Prepare a graph on copy paper with columns labeled *red, yellow, orange, green, brown,* and *blue.* Leave a space below each color word and label it *total*. Make one copy of the graph for each student. Fill a bowl with candy-covered chocolates and place a small scoop near the bowl. Each student should take one scoop of candies and place them on a napkin beside his graph. Have students sort their candies by color and then arrange them in the appropriate columns on their graphs. Finally, have students count the candies in each column and record the numbers under the column labels in the space marked *total*. Provide crayons or markers. Let students remove the candies one at a time and replace them with matching circles. When a student is finished coloring his graph, let him enjoy a candy treat!

Number Cookies 👓 1²3 ∴

Gather a supply of number-shaped cookie cutters, chocolate chips or candy-covered chocolates, and refrigerated sugar cookie dough. Roll out the dough on a sheet of waxed paper and let each student use a cookie cutter to cut out a number cookie. Then, have each student count and place the corresponding number of chocolate chips or candies on her cookie. Bake the cookies according to package directions. When cooled, let students enjoy a snack!

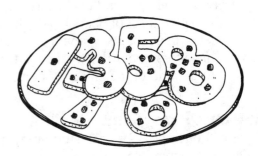

Do the Jelly Bean Jump 👓 1²3

Cut out a class supply of large jelly bean shapes from colorful paper. Label each jelly bean with a number from 0 to 10 and laminate them for durability. Place the jelly beans on the floor in a large circle. Play lively music and have students walk around the perimeter of the ring of jelly beans. Stop the music and have each student stop where he is. Call a student's name and have him pick up the jelly bean closest to him. Have him identify the number on his jelly bean and lead the class in jumping up and down that many times while counting aloud. Continue playing until all of the students have turns leading the class in the jelly bean jump.

Cookie Jar Game

Copy a class supply of the Cookie Patterns (page 63) on colorful paper and number the cookies sequentially. Cut out the cookies and laminate them for durability. Put the cookies in a cookie jar. To play, have students sit in a circle on the floor and let each student take a cookie from the jar. Have the class recite the following chant with you. Continue playing until all of the cookies have been returned to the cookie jar.

Who Took the Cookie from the Cookie Jar?
Class: Who took the cookie from the cookie jar?
Teacher: Number _____ took the cookie from the cookie jar.
Student Whose Number Is Called: Who me?
(The student holds up his cookie and shows the number written on it, then rushes to put it back in the cookie jar.)
Class: Yes, you.
Student: Couldn't be.
Class: Then, who?
Student: Number _____ took the cookie from the cookie jar.

Note: Start the game by selecting the first number to call out. For subsequent rounds, the last student to have her number called will select the next student by choosing a number. If desired, write all of the numbers on the board and cross them out as they are used so that students will know which numbers are still available as the game continues.

Tasty Teddy Bear Treats

Make 10 copies of the Bear Pattern (page 71) on light brown paper. Cut out and laminate the bears for durability. Draw a large honey pot on the board. Give each student a paper or plastic bowl to represent a honey pot and at least 10 bear-shaped graham crackers on a napkin. Use tape or magnets to display a set of bears inside the honey pot on the board. Have each student make a matching set of bear-shaped graham crackers in their own "honey pots." After students complete their sets, have them pour the crackers back onto their napkins. Repeat with a new set for students to match. At the end of the game, students can enjoy a tasty treat.

Going on a Honey Hunt

Prepare a "honey pot" for each student by gluing a border of yellow construction paper around the top of a small paper bag. Label each bag with a student's name and place a blank square of paper inside. Make a bear headband for each student by attaching two brown paper semicircle ears to a strip of poster board or sturdy paper. Staple the headbands to fit around each student's head. Fill a class supply of snack-sized resealable plastic bags with 5–10 pieces of honey-flavored cereal each and hide the bags around the room. Let each student put on her headband and carry her honey pot as she hunts for a bag of treats. Have students return to their seats when they find "honey" and count the pieces of cereal in their bags. Let students write the totals on their pieces of paper. Then, invite students to enjoy the treats. (Provide extras for students who had fewer pieces in their bags.)

Cookie Patterns

Activities found on pages 61–62.

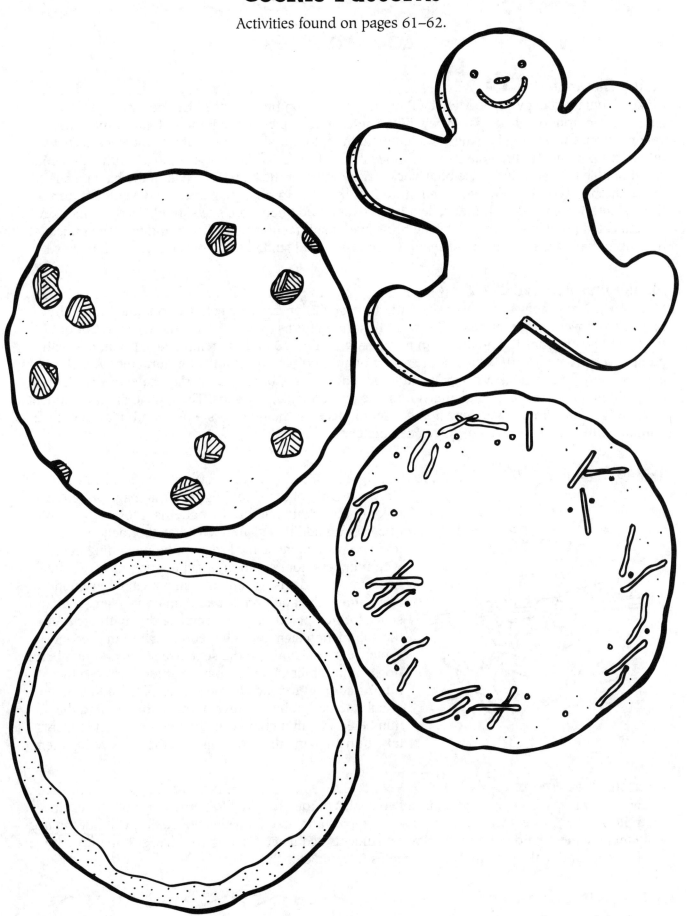

Zoo Animals

Going Bananas 👀 1²3 +/- ....

Make an enlarged copy of the Monkey Pattern (page 67) on brown paper. Cut out the pattern and glue it to the front of a large paper bag. Make at least 40 copies of the Banana Pattern (page 67) on yellow paper. Cut out the bananas and laminate them for durability. Program 22 index cards with numbers from 0 to 10. Program 22 more index cards, 11 with addition signs and 11 with subtraction signs. Shuffle the cards and place both stacks facedown near the bag. Place half of the banana cutouts inside the bag and place the other half in front of the bag. To play the game, have a student turn over the top card in each stack. If the student turns over an addition sign, she should "feed the monkey" the indicated number of bananas; if she turns over a subtraction sign, she should take the indicated number of bananas from the monkey. Play continues until students run out of cards or bananas.

Monkeying Around 👀 ∴ 🎲 ....

Make an enlarged copy of the Monkey Pattern (page 67) on brown paper. Cut out and attach the monkey to a piece of poster board. Copy 22 Banana Patterns (page 67) on yellow paper. Cut out the bananas. Program 11 bananas with numbers from 0 to 10 and the remaining 11 bananas with number sets from 0 to 10. Laminate the poster board and banana cutouts for durability. Attach hook-and-loop tape to the monkey's hands and to the backs of the bananas. To play, have one student choose a numbered banana and attach it to one of the monkey's hands. Then, have another student find the banana with the matching number set to place on the monkey's other hand. Play continues until all of the numbers and sets have been matched.

Tricky Tree Frogs +/- ....

Copy a supply of the Tree Frog Patterns (page 68) on colorful paper and cut out the patterns. Program four frogs, one with an addition sign, one with a subtraction sign, and two with equal signs. Program the remaining frogs with numbers from addition or subtraction facts. Create two game boards using sentence strips. On one sentence strip, attach the addition sign and an equal sign, leaving space for numbered frogs to complete the math fact. Attach the subtraction sign and other equal sign to the second sentence strip. Laminate the sentence strips and numbered frogs for durability. To play, have a student choose two numbered frogs to place in the spaces of the addition or subtraction problem. Have another student find the numbered frog that completes the math fact. Let students take turns making the problems and then answering them.

Colorful Tree Frogs ABAB 🎲 ⊙⊙ ....

Choose several colors of paper and make two copies of the Tree Frog Patterns (page 68) on each color. Repeat the process with a reduced set of copies and an enlarged set of copies. Cut out the frogs and laminate them for durability. To play, let students sequence the frogs by size, sort the frogs by color or size, and make patterns for classmates to complete.

Something Is Fishy

Make 10 enlarged copies of the Seal Pattern (page 69) on colorful paper. Program each seal with a number from 1 to 10. Cut out and laminate the seals for durability. Give each student a small paper plate and a handful of fish-shaped crackers. Tell each student to put her crackers in a pile on one side of her plate. Display a seal for students to see. Have students identify the number on the seal, count that number of fish-shaped crackers, and create matching sets in the centers of their plates. Repeat for the other seal cutouts. When the activity is complete, allow students to enjoy their "seal snacks."

Penguin Counting Song

Have students move like penguins while singing this silly song. As the class sings each verse together, encourage students to "splash," "flap their flippers," "swim," "dance," etc., like penguins.

Penguin Counting Song
(Sing to the tune of "The Twelve Days of Christmas.")

I went to the South Pole and what did I see?
One little penguin swimming.

Continue with:

Two penguins splashing
Three penguins flapping
Four penguins dancing
Five penguins hopping
Six penguins playing
Seven penguins waddling

Eight penguins bathing
Nine penguins diving
Ten penguins sliding
Eleven penguins fishing
Twelve penguins napping

Note: If students only know numbers from 1 to 10, stop singing after the 10th verse.

Leo Lion Says . . .

Play a "roaring" version of Simon Says while encouraging movement and counting skills. Explain that students should listen carefully and perform the suggested actions, but only when the instruction begins, "Leo Lion says . . ." If students do not hear this phrase, they should stay still. If desired, make a list of actions before starting the game. Remember, instructions should include counting activities. Example instructions include, "Leo Lion says hop three times," "Leo Lion says clap 10 times," and "Leo Lion says touch your toes four times."

Silly Snakes

Using a permanent marker, draw snake facial features on one handle of each of two jump ropes. Have students stand in a circle. Place the jump ropes on the floor in the middle of the circle. Ask students to take turns making "snake shapes" by manipulating the jump ropes to form circles, squares, rectangles, triangles, and other familiar shapes. When a student finishes forming a shape, have the rest of the students call out the name of the shape. Then, let two students make shapes at the same time and have the rest of the students compare the two shapes. Are they the same? If they are different, how? Are they the same size? Which shape has more angles?

Counting Kangaroos ✏️ 1st +/-

Make one copy of the Kangaroo Pattern (page 70) on light brown paper for each student. Give each student a pattern to cut out. Assign each student a number and let him write it on his kangaroo. Help students as needed. (If students only know numbers from 1 to 10 and there are more than 10 students in the class, divide the class into two groups and let each group make numbered kangaroos from 1 to 10.) Have students attach the kangaroos in numerical order along a wall to make a number line. Write addition and subtraction facts on index cards. Let students take turns selecting a card and solving the math fact by hopping along the number line to find the answer.

Kangaroo Peekaboo 👀 ∴ 🎲

Make 11 copies of the Kangaroo Pattern (page 70) and 11 copies of the Joey Pattern (page 70) on light brown paper. Cut out all of the kangaroos and joeys. Program the kangaroos' pockets with number sets from 0 to 10. Program the joeys with numbers from 0 to 10. Laminate all of the kangaroos and joeys for durability. Cut a slit along each kangaroo's pouch to create a pocket. Have students work in pairs to match the sets and numbers by sliding each joey into the correct kangaroo's pouch.

Dressed Up Bears 👀 ∴ 🎲

Make a class set of the Bear Pattern (page 71) on brown paper. Program each bear with a number set. (If students only know numbers from 1 to 10 and there are more than 10 students in the class, make two sets of bears with numbers from 1 to 10.) Make a class set of the T-Shirt Pattern (page 71) on colorful paper and program each shirt with a number to match one of the bear patterns. Cut out the bears and T-shirts and laminate them for durability. During circle time, give each student a bear. Spread the shirts on the floor in the middle of the circle. Have students take turns finding the T-shirts that match the sets on the bears.

Bear Laundry 👀 1²3

Obtain a small plastic basket that resembles a laundry basket. Attach a piece of hook-and-loop tape to the side of the basket. Make 10 copies of the Bear Pattern (page 71) on brown paper. Program each bear with a number from 1 to 10. Make at least 10 copies of the T-Shirt Pattern (page 71) on colorful paper. Cut out the bears and T-shirts and laminate them for durability. Attach a piece of hook-and-loop tape to the back of each bear. To play the game, have a student attach a bear pattern to the laundry basket and then count and place the matching number of T-shirts inside the basket. Students can play this game with partners, as well.

Monkey & Banana Patterns

Activities found on page 64.

CD-104199 *It's Number Time!*

Tree Frog Patterns

Activities found on page 64.

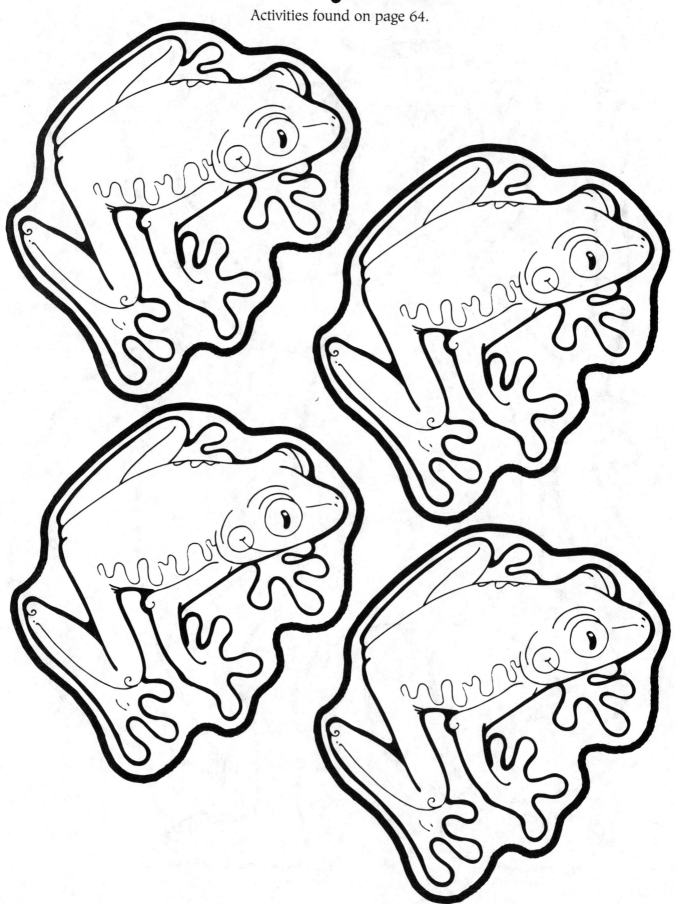

Seal Pattern

Activity found on page 65.

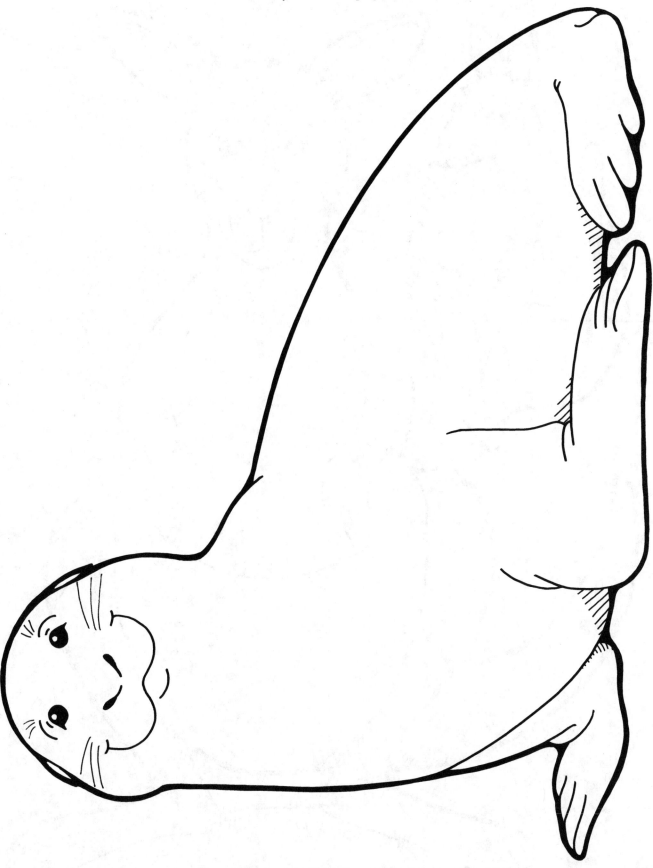

CD-104199 *It's Number Time!*

Kangaroo & Joey Patterns

Activities found on page 66.

CD-104199 *It's Number Time!*

Bear & T-Shirt Patterns

Activities found on pages 62 & 66.

CD-104199 *It's Number Time!*

General Number Activities: Buttons

Button Necklaces  ABAB ....

Cut a class supply of pieces of yarn to use for necklaces. Wrap a small piece of cellophane tape around one end of each piece of yarn to make it easier for students to string buttons. Provide an assortment of large buttons in two or three colors. Program index cards with simple patterns of colorful circles that match the colors of the buttons. Have a student choose a card and then thread the corresponding colors of buttons on her yarn to make a pattern. Have her repeat the pattern a number of times to make a series. When finished, help the student tie the ends of her yarn together to make a necklace.

Button Graphs ABAB 1²3 ||| ✏ ....

Prepare a graph on copy paper with four or five columns labeled with color words. Leave a space below each color word and label it *total*. Make one copy of the graph for each student. Fill a bowl with buttons in the colors that correspond to the graph labels. Each student should take one handful of buttons and place them beside his graph. Have each student sort the buttons by color and then arrange them in the appropriate columns on the graph. Finally, have students count the buttons in each column and record the numbers under the column labels in the space marked *total*. Provide crayons or markers. Let students remove the buttons one at a time and replace them with matching circles.

Button Puzzle Cards 1²3 +/- 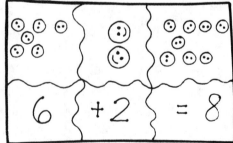 ....

Program addition and subtraction facts horizontally across the bottoms of several large index cards. Above each number in the problems, attach small sets of buttons that represent the numbers. Cut the cards into puzzle pieces by separating them into three pieces for younger students or six pieces for older students. Be sure to cut the puzzles unevenly so that as students fit the pieces together, the pieces will only fit with the correctly matching pieces. To play, have a student mix up the pieces of two or three puzzles and then work to assemble the puzzles correctly. For a challenge, keep the puzzle pieces with the answers on them separate from the rest of the pieces. Have students first assemble the math problems, solve them, and then check their answers by completing the puzzles with the answer pieces.

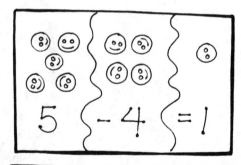

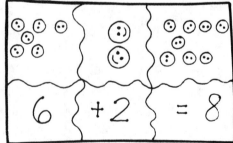

Button Hole Sorting ABAB
Fill a resealable plastic bag with a collection of buttons that have one, two, or four holes. Make sorting cards by drawing a picture of each type of button on an index card. Place the cards inside the bag with the buttons. To play, a student should empty the bag onto her desk, spread the cards in front of her, and sort the buttons onto the cards according to the number of holes. If desired, challenge students to time themselves to see how fast they can sort the buttons. Then, let them try to beat their own best times. You can also create a class set of bags of buttons so that the whole class can play the game at the same time.

Button Counting 123
Program a class supply of large index cards with numbers from 1 to 10. Have students sit in a circle on the floor. Place 10 clear plastic containers labeled from 1 to 10 in the middle of the circle. Put a container of buttons and the stack of index cards nearby. Let students take turns going to the center of the circle, drawing a card, and counting that number of buttons into the correct plastic container. As a student counts the buttons, the class should count aloud with him. Continue playing until all of the students have turns.

Mr. Buttons 123 ABAB
Make a simple puppet by sewing buttons onto a tube sock to make facial features. Introduce the puppet to the class as "Mr. Buttons." Slip the puppet onto your hand and plunge Mr. Buttons into a container of buttons to grab a mouthful. Drop the buttons on a table and have students count in unison to determine how many buttons Mr. Buttons grabbed in his mouth. Let students take turns using Mr. Buttons. Students can also use Mr. Buttons to practice sorting and making patterns.

Pattern Experts ABAB
Provide construction paper, pencils or crayons, and a bowl of buttons. Use buttons to start a pattern on a piece of construction paper and have a student continue it. Then, have the student name the pattern with letters and write the letters below the buttons on the construction paper. For example, the repetition of a red button and a blue button would be written as *ABAB*. Finally, challenge the student to translate the pattern. Remove the buttons, leaving only the letter pattern written on the piece of paper. Have the student choose different buttons to place on the paper in the same type of pattern. For example, a student might create a repeating pattern of a yellow button followed by a green button for a different representation of *ABAB*.

General Number Activities: Calendar

Calendar Patterns ⏱ ABAB

Use seasonal, geometric, or colorful calendar cover-ups to reinforce patterning skills. Each day, place a cover-up on the calendar to create a simple pattern. For example, during the month of April you might alternate a raindrop cover-up and an umbrella cover-up. When students have identified the pattern, allow them to express the pattern in different ways as the next day's cover-up is added. For example, students might make a soft clap on a "raindrop day" and a loud clap on an "umbrella day." If desired, allow students to take turns adding the cover-up each day. Also, consider changing the pattern every week or every other week instead of using the same pattern for the entire month.

Calendar Treats ⏱ 🍬 🔢

This is a great activity to do after lunch. Use a tube of icing to draw a calendar on a large pan of brownies or sheet cake. Draw grid lines and number the squares from 1 to 30 (or 31). Cut the brownies or cake into squares along the grid lines. Place a set of cards labeled from 1 to 30 (or 31) in a container. Have each student draw a card, identify the date shown, and find the matching number square on the brownie calendar. Help each student remove her square from the tray, place it on a plate, and take it to her seat to enjoy.

Personal Calendars ⏱ 1st ✏️

Let students practice their number writing. At the beginning of each month, prepare a blank calendar grid. To help students know the starting and ending days for each month, place Xs in the unused squares. (For example, if the month starts on a Tuesday and ends on a Thursday, draw Xs in the first Sunday and Monday squares and in the last Friday and Saturday squares.) Give each student a copy of the calendar and instruct him to write in the numbers beginning with the first empty square. If students have not learned to write numbers through 30 or 31, write in the numbers they do not know before copying the calendar. Leave the squares blank for the numbers they are able to fill in. Students can take their calendars home to post in their rooms.

Weather Trackers

Each day, have students determine the weather conditions outside and place the appropriate cover-up (rain, cloud, sun, snow, etc.) on the classroom calendar. At the end of each week, have students count aloud to determine how many days were rainy, cloudy, sunny, snowy, etc. For a challenge at the end of the month, have students count all of the days of each type of weather and compare the totals to determine which type of weather occurred most often during the month.

Let's Have Order 1st

Post a blank calendar grid on the wall. Hang numbered calendar cover-ups on all of the Sundays and Saturdays and leave the other days blank. Have a student or small group of students work to fill in each week with the appropriate cover-ups. For younger students, consider filling in a few more spaces on the calendar to help them check their work.

Calendar Counting 1²3

Use this activity each time a new monthly calendar is posted in the classroom. Have students count a variety of things using the calendar display, such as the number of Saturdays, the number of birthdays and holidays, or the number of special class events. If desired, have the class count aloud together or have students work in small groups to determine the answers.

Play Peekaboo 1st

Cover several of the dates on the classroom calendar with self-stick notes. Choose a student to guess one of the covered numbers and then remove the self-stick note to check his answer. Use this activity with the whole class and select volunteers to guess the numbers. Or, let students play this game in small groups with one student acting as the teacher and choosing the numbers to cover. Other group members can then try to guess the covered numbers.

General Number Activities: Counting

Number Punch 1²3 👀 ∴

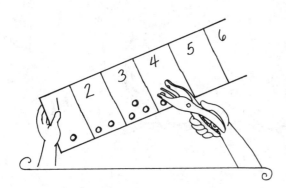

Program a sentence strip for each student by dividing the strip into 10 sections and numbering each one. The sections for the higher numbers should be larger than the sections for the smaller numbers. Place the sentence strips and several hole punchers on a table. To complete the activity, each student should take a sentence strip, read the numbers, and punch the corresponding number of holes in the spaces. For a challenge, write the numbers in random order. If younger students have trouble punching holes in sentence strips, use strips of thinner paper instead.

Shipshape 1²3 👀 ✎

Cut out a large circle, square, rectangle, and triangle from construction paper. Glue the shapes onto a piece of poster board to make a game board. Program a supply of index cards with shapes and numbers. Each card should display one number and one shape. Laminate the game board and cards for durability. Provide a bowl of counters. To play, students should place the cards facedown in a stack. Students should take turns choosing a card and placing the correct number of counters on top of the corresponding shape on the game board. For example, if a student selects a card with a circle and a 4 on it, she would place four counters on top of the circle on the game board.

Connecting the Dots 1²3 1st

Make a set of large number cards that can easily be seen from across the room. Give the cards to several students and have them scatter around the classroom or a designated area. Choose a student to walk in sequence to each classmate holding a number card. All of the students should count aloud as the student moves from number to number. To "connect the dots" and create a classroom design, give the student a ball of yarn. As she walks from student to student in sequence, have each student hold the yarn as she brings it to him. A path of yarn will show the sequence in which she arrived at each number card. To collect the yarn, she can rewind it as she works backward through the number sequence.

Roll & Count 1²3 . . . .

Have students stand in a circle. Provide a pair of large, foam fair number cubes. (For younger students, provide only one cube.) Choose a student to roll the cubes. Have him count aloud the number of dots shown and choose a simple exercise, such as toe touches or jumping jacks. The student should lead the class in performing the exercise that number of times while everyone counts aloud. Continue playing until all of the students have had a chance to roll the cubes and lead the activity.

Growing Patterns 1²3 ABAB . . . .

Provide 10 paper bowls or plates and 55 counters. Number the bowls from 1 to 10. Have a student place one counter in the first bowl. Explain to students that they will create a pattern that always grows by one. Ask students to determine how many counters should be in the second bowl. Invite another student to place two counters in that bowl. Have students continue the pattern until all of the bowls have counters in them. When the pattern is complete, let students experiment with other growing patterns and alternating patterns.

Rhythmic Counting 1²3 . . . .

Combine music and math to create a unique counting game. Distribute a variety of instruments to students. Then, encourage counting by asking students to play their instruments a specific number of times. Choose student volunteers to play their instruments while the class counts along. For a listening challenge, call out a type of instrument and a number so that only students with that instrument play the specified number of times. Continue calling instruments and numbers to create a "number song."

Human Numbers 1²3 ⊙⊙ ✎ ∴ . . . .

Have small groups of students lie on the floor in configurations to create numbers from 1 to 10. Photograph each "human number" the class creates. Attach the pictures to large sheets of paper. Let students surround each photo with sets of stickers, stamps, or small drawings that also represent the number. Laminate the pages and bind them into a class number book to display in a classroom library or math center.

Suggested Literature List

3, 2, 1 Go! A Transportation Countdown by Sarah L. Schuette (Capstone Press, 2003)

10 Button Book by William Accorsi (Workman Publishing Company, 1999)

12 Ways to Get to 11 by Eve Merriam (Aladdin, 1996)

The 100th Day of School by Angela Shelf Medearis (Cartwheel, 1996)

Anno's Counting Book by Mitsumasa Anno (HarperTrophy, 1986)

Around the Year: A Calendar and Counting Rhyme by Christina Goodings (Lion, 2002)

Blast-Off: A Space Counting Book by Norma Cole (Charlesbridge Publishing, 1994)

Chicka Chicka 1, 2, 3 by Bill Martin, Jr., and Michael Sampson (Simon & Schuster Children's
    Publishing, 2004)

Circus 1-2-3 by Megan Halsey (HarperCollins, 2000)

Count-a-saurus by Nancy Blumenthal (Aladdin, 1992)

Counting Farm by Kathy Henderson (Candlewick, 1998)

Count on Clifford by Norman Bridwell (Scholastic, 1987)

Curious George and the Birthday Surprise by Margret Rey and H. A. Rey (Houghton Mifflin, 2003)

The Doorbell Rang by Pat Hutchins (HarperTrophy, 1989)

Farm Counting Book by Jane Miller (Little Simon, 1992)

Fish Eyes: A Book You Can Count On by Lois Ehlert (Voyager Books, 1992)

Five Little Monkeys Jumping on the Bed by Eileen Christelow (Clarion Books, 1989)

Grandma's Button Box by Linda Williams Aber (Kane Press, 2002)

Happy Birthday to You! (Classic Seuss) by Dr. Seuss (Random House Books for Young Readers, 1959)

How Do Dinosaurs Count to Ten? by Jane Yolen (Blue Sky Press, 2004)

The Icky Bug Counting Book by Jerry Pallotta (Charlesbridge Publishing, 1992)

Miss Bindergarten Celebrates the 100th Day of Kindergarten by Joseph Slate (Puffin, 2002)

Mouse Count by Ellen Stoll Walsh (Voyager Books, 1995)

On the Launch Pad: A Counting Book About Rockets by Michael Dahl (Picture Window Books, 2004)

Over in the Meadow by Ezra Jack Keats (Puffin, 1999)

How Many Snails? A Counting Book by Paul Giganti (HarperTrophy, 1994)

Seasons 1 2 3 by Patricia Whitehouse (Heinemann, 2002)

Ten Little Ladybugs by Melanie Gerth (Piggy Toes Press, 2001)

Ten Little Rabbits by Virginia Grossman (Chronicle Books, LLC, 1995)

Trucks at Work: A Counting Pop-Up by Frank Ansley (Little Simon, 1997)

Turtle Splash! Countdown at the Pond by Cathryn Falwell (Greenwillow, 2001)

The Twelve Circus Rings by Seymour Chwast (Harcourt, 1993)

Two Ways to Count to Ten: A Liberian Folk Tale retold by Ruby Dee (Henry Holt and Co., 1990)

Under the Sea 1, 2, 3: Counting Ocean Life by Barbara Knox (Capstone Press, 2003)

The Very Hungry Caterpillar by Eric Carle (Scholastic, 1994)

When Sheep Cannot Sleep: The Counting Book by Satoshi Kitamura (Farrar, Straus and Giroux, 1988)

You Can Count at the Ocean by David Brooks (Northwood Press, 2005)

Index of Activities by Skill

Index of Activities by Skill